A WINTER IN

BELFAST

NORTHERN IRELAND
26th November 1976 – 16th March 1977

D Company 2nd Battalion The Parachute Regiment

Belfast: Clonard, Falls, Ballymurphy, Whiterock.

Together With Recollections From Those Who Were There

By Lieutenant

David Ellis

The Parachute Regiment

Dedicated to Corporal Stephen Prior & Corporal Paul Sullivan.
Killed in action at Goose Green, Falkland Islands.

CONTENTS

With thanks to Philip Russell, Michael Emberson, Keith Donkin, David Smith, Peter Akister, Warwick Stacey, David Benest, Graham Benton and Nick O'Connor for their recollections, and of course all in 10 Platoon. Thanks to Thomas Mountney for colouring photographs.

i

INTRODUCTION

This diary was written on each day throughout the tour. It sat unread by me or indeed anyone else apart from my father from the end of the tour until 2019 when I started to read it again. I felt that it is a story that should be told.

There are one or two events that were described to me at the time by the Toms and they may be slightly embellished but who wants to ruin a good story? Other sources included the daily logs and NIREP produced by Brigade Headquarters.

I have included comments from some officers, NCOs and soldiers who were there at time. I have not pulled punches when discussing certain officers; most, however, were decent men doing their best.

I have mentioned incidents outside 2 PARA's area in order to give an appreciation of how much was going on in the Province in those days. I have omitted routine assaults, most small bomb hoaxes and so on from my diary when I was writing it. The tour was, compared to earlier tours, relatively quiet and by the grace of God, good training and the spirit of the Regiment we had no fatalities.

Much has been written about The Parachute Regiment in Northern Ireland, not all of it flattering but we were not all lunatics and psychopaths. Unlike the terrorists we did not set out in the morning intending to kill and maim men, women and children. None of us came home to parades with bands playing or to a hero's welcome; we slipped off trains, buses or aircraft and disappeared into barracks. No one wore uniform in public in those days due to the risk of assassination by the IRA. We were not regarded by anyone as heroes and I am not bothered by that. The dead were shipped back home in the holds of aircraft both civilian and military and there were no special ceremonies at RAF Lyneham. The wounded were treated in the military hospital system in Northern Ireland and then sent back to one of several military hospitals on the mainland. All closed down now. No Help for Heroes then. I'm not bitter, we treat our blokes much better nowadays and so it should be.

We were, of course, not officially at war, however a bar to the General Service Medal 1962 was issued to anyone who had served 30 days or more in theatre. If you were killed or injured before your thirty days were up you were still awarded the medal and clasp. I wear mine with pride.

There are words below that might offend. Don't be offended, that's how it was in those days.

This story is written based on my diary as I saw it at the time and with the help of those who were there. It is a work of non-fiction. No names have been changed and no events described are made up.

The views expressed here are the author's own and should not be taken as indicative of the views of The Parachute Regiment, the Ministry of Defence or any other British Government agency.

PART 1

THE MEN, THE AREA, THE MISSION

<u>D Company Orbat (Order of Battle) as at Nov. 1976</u>

Coy HQ

O.C. Maj. Ben Hodgson (49)
2 i/c Capt Mark Whitford (49a)
CSM WO2 Duncan (49b)
CQMS C/Sgt Jimmy Kerr (49c)
L/Cpl Michael Emberson (Int.)
L/Cpl Don Jones (Int.)
Pte Ian Taylor (OC's bodyguard)

Plus various signallers, cooks, bottle washers, drivers etc. whose names I have forgotten.

10 PLATOON

Lt David Ellis C/S 41L
Sgt Don MacNaughton
Cpl Blowers
Cpl Robinson
L/Cpl Gibbins
L/Cpl Camp
L/Cpl Bell
L/Cpl Sullivan. (KIA Falklands)

11 PLATOON
Lt Peter Akister C/S 42L
Sgt Edwards
Cpl Young
Cpl Squires
Cpl Johnson
L/Cpl Doolan
L/Cpl Brian
L/Cpl O'Connell MM

12 PLATOON
2/Lt Warwick 'Abo' Stacey C/S 43L
Sgt Phil Evans
Cpl Rooster Barber
Cpl Grey
L/Cpl Bland
L/Cpl Jeanette
L/Cpl Jones
L/Cpl Elliot

(Versus C2 PIRA)

10 Platoon Orbat

Lt David Ellis

Sgt Don MacNaughton

1 SECTION 41A
Cpl John Robinson
Pte Steve Anderton
Pte Steve Prior (KIA Falklands)
Pte Smith 28
L/Cpl Mick Gibbins
Pte Steve Sharpe
Pte Michael Connelly
Pte Fleming

2 SECTION 41B
Cpl Windy Blowers
Pte Gammon
Pte Geoff Hough
Pte Gordon Fawcett
L/Cpl Paul Sullivan (KIA Falklands)
Pte Chris Adams
Pte McAteer
Pte Martin Magerison
Pte Reid
Pte Stewart

3 SECTION 41C
L/Cpl Tom Camp
Pte David Smith 95
Pte Mortonson
Pte Keith Donkin
L/Cpl John Bell
Pte Spence
Pte Ware
Pte Allen
Pte Perryman
L/Cpl Jones

Lt. David Ellis

Cpl John Robinson's patrol.
Pte "Billy" Connolly, Pte M. Lowry RCT, n/k RUC, Cpl John Robinson, Pte
Steve Sharpe, Dave Smith, Paddy Fleming & Constable Macfarlane.

North Howard St yard. CQMS Jimmy Kerr approaching, probably wants some
kit off me. Or to sell porn.

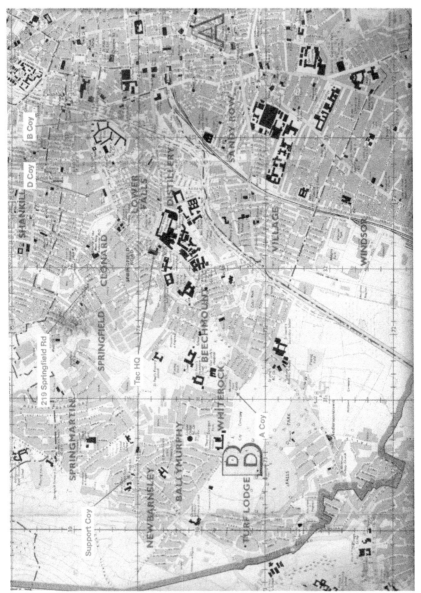

2 PARA Company locations.

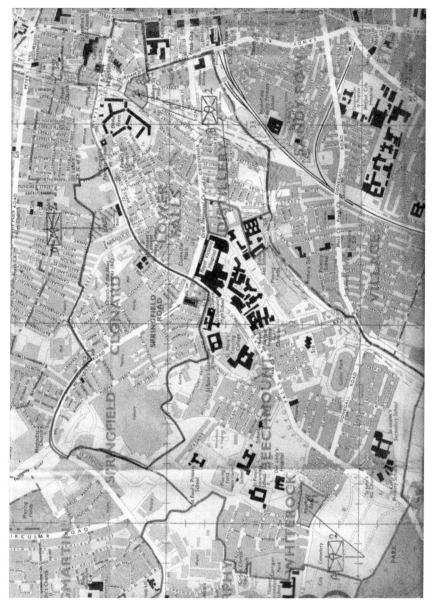

'Tribal Map' - Orange is Loyalist, Green is Republican.

The Clonard, Our Patch

The locals, almost entirely Catholic and therefore Republican, appear to have been told to avoid provoking us. One kid got the boot put in for slagging a patrol. Some will talk to us.

The area is made up mainly of terraced houses and the Mackies factory, the second largest employer in NI. There are very few derelicts, N of the peace line the area is almost entirely derelict, the result of rioting in the early '70s.There are some new houses, mainly in the Beechmount area. The roads are generally short and straight, laid out at right angles. There are plenty of good sniper positions.

Other features: Falls Rd, Springfield Rd, RVH (Royal Victoria Hospital), 219 Springfield Rd base, Clonard monastery.

North Howard St Mill

The accommodation is quite good (by NI standards). We occupy 3 floors of the mill. Officers have a room each for a change, the Toms one per section. There is a combined Officers / SNCOs mess, a cinema and a gym in a bunker on the square. All has been redecorated recently.

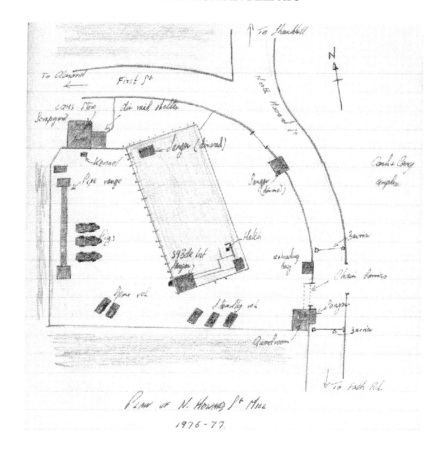

Summary of the Intelligence Brief to 2 PARA from 2 Light Infantry

The main threat in the area comes from C Company 2 PIRA known locally as C2. There is a hard core of a dozen or more and the majority of these have had experience in bombings, shootings, hijacking, robbery etc. All have been interned at some period during the troubles. As stated, apart from the anniversary of Internment the area has been relatively quiet. It is possible that the Clonard is used for planning, preparing and staging through operations to other parts of the city. A recent bombing in a chemist's shop in the University area left traces of a type of bomb used by C2 in the past. This could indicate that C2 are involved in the making and transportation of bombs to pre-designated targets.

Also we must consider the possibility of attacks on SF, C2 have the capability to mount a single shot sniper attack, ambush or booby trap bomb.

It was during the anniversary of Internment that the area was most active, this was between 8-10 Aug '76. There were six shooting incidents and one bombing/shooting when SF sustained three casualties. Since then the area has been relatively quiet with only four shooting incidents, SF being involved in only one of these. Also during the anniversary there was general rioting involving hijacks, petrol bombings and aggro.

Finally the enemy propaganda machine, in the form of the Provisional Sinn Fein will pounce upon any situation, in some cases stage managed to make the Army look ridiculous, oppressive, or seem to be harassing locals. In some cases it would appear that they have a direct line to the City Desk of the 'Irish Press'.

Operations

The Light Infantry appear a bit slack, end-of-tour-itis. Poor patrolling techniques, i.e. walking over open spaces, not covering each other etc. We need to lean more on the PIRA (Provisional IRA); more stopping and searching is needed.

The Fusilier shot yesterday (Wed) was hit in the throat by a ricochet. Round fired from about 300m. DOA (dead on arrival) at Musgrave.

Ben's main O Group in the morning. Covered all aspects of the coming months.

- Mission: Work together with the RUC in order to maintain law and order to enable a political settlement to take place.
- Execution: Continue attrition of PIRA. Neutralise other subversive organisations. Assist RUC to return to all areas of the

city. Establish good community relations. Set up specific community relations projects.

- Tasks: Using a three day cycle we will operate by taking the following commitments. Patrols, Standby, Guard.

Patrols platoon:

Provide continuous coverage on the ground except 0200 to 0630.

2 x 4 man in daylight commanded by a Cpl or L/Cpl.

3 x 4 man in the evening commanded by an officer or Sgt.

Must be mutually supporting. Stop and search cars & personnel especially known baddies. Be curious.

Standby platoon:

Standby 1. (Playboy)

Section of 8 in two Pigs or Landrovers. Must be leaving base within two minutes of being called out. Sleep in standby room. Fully dressed, weapons to hand. Must eat and wash together. War kit to stay in the Pigs. No beer.

Commander to stay in the ops room.

Tasks: Immediate reaction for VCPs (vehicle check points) and arrests.

Standby 2. (Mayfair)

Ten minutes to move. Stay in section or Wog Shop (canteen) floor. Fully dressed, kit to hand. Take over as standby 1 if standby 1 moves out. May drink beer.

Tasks: Pre planned ops such as cordons, lifts etc.

Standby 3. (Mayfair)

Thirty minutes notice. Provide 2 x 4 patrol 0200 to 0630 for two and a half hours to rest patrols. Standby for OP duty.

STANDBY SECTION
TUES 1300 to WED 1300
41A and 41D.

Pte	PRIOR.	1300 to 1530. *	0130 to 0300 †	
Pte	SMITH 28	1530 to 1800 *	0300 to 0530 †	
Pte	SHARPE	1800 to 2030 *	0530 to 0800 †	
Pte	FLEMING	2030 to 2300 *	0800 to 1030 †	
Pte	ANDERTON	2300 to 0130 *†	1030 to 1300 *†	

* STAND DOWN PERIOD   † OPs ROOM RUNNER PERIOD †

NOTE:

ALL PERSONEL ARE ON IMMEDIATE STANDBY FOR THE FULL 24 HR PERIOD EXCEPT FOR THE PERIODS SHOWN ABOVE.

NOTES:

A. DRESS. ALL PERSONS ON STANDBY WILL BE DRESSED AT ALL TIMES, IN THEIR ROOM. i.e. BOOTS, PUTTEES, DENIMS/OG'S, SMOCK WITH THE REMAINDER OF THEIR KIT BY THEIR BEDS READY TO MOVE.

B. LOCATION. ALL PERSONEL ON STANDBY WILL REMAIN IN THEIR ROOM. THEY MAY GO TO THE NOG SHOP OR TOILET, BUT THEY WILL INFORM SOMEONE ELSE ON STANDBY WHO IS REMAINING IN THE ROOM. TWO PEOPLE WILL REMAIN IN THE ROOM AT ANY ONE TIME. PERSONS GOING TO THE NOG SHOP/TOILET WILL RETURN TO THEIR ROOM AS SOON AS POSSIBLE. NO HANGING AROUNDS IN THE NOG SHOP. THE T.V. ROOM AND CINEMA IS OUT OF BOUNDS TO ALL PERSONEL ON STANDBY FOR THE 24 HR PERIOD. EXCEPT FOR CLEANING PURPOSES.

C. MEALS. ALL PERSONEL ON STANDBY WILL GO TO MEALS EN BULK AT THE EARLIST OPPORTUNITY OR REMAIN IN THE ROOM.

ALL PERSONEL ARE MAKE SURE THAT THEY FULLY COMPLY WITH THE ABOVE RULES. ANY PERSON WHO FOUND NOT COMPLYING WITH THESES ORDERS WILL BE DEALT WITH SEVERLY. ANY QUESTIONS ABOUT THE STAND BY, ASK EITHER CPL ROBINSON OR LCPL GIBBINS. MAKE SURE THAT YOU FULLY UNDERSTAND THESE ORDERS, IGNORANCE WILL NOT BE EXCEPTED AS AN EXCUSE.

JnRobinson.
CPL ROBINSON JM.

Pte	PRIOR	
Pte	SMITH 28	
Pte	SHARPE	
Pte	FLEMING	
Pte	ANDERTON	

Cpl John Robinson's Orders for the Standby Section.
With thanks to Steve Sharpe.

Guard platoon:

3 + 9 Guard for NHS St (North Howard St) base.

2 + 4 Guard for telephone exchange.

3 stood by for RVH to guard SF, terrorists or VIP casualties.

Internal escorts.

Fatigues as required.

Platoon commanders and Sgts. to do duty in the Ops Room when their platoon is on guard.

PART 2

THE DIARY OF EVENTS FROM

26TH NOVEMBER 1976 TO

16TH MARCH 1977

Advance Party

Friday 26th November

0300. Chalk parade on Montgomery Square, Aldershot. Raining! Brigadier Howlett came to say goodbye. Eventually arrived at RAF Lyneham, had a good RAF breakfast. Hung around. Mounted C-130 at about 0730. Drove around and took off at 0815.

Arrived Aldergrove 0915. Raining.

Arrived North Howard St 1020. The less said about the move the better.

1400 – 1630 on patrol.

1900 – 2100 on patrol.

Saturday 27th November

Day spent getting organised, unpacking, sorting weapons and ammo etc. The main body of the advance party arriving by LSL was delayed due to bad weather.

1800 – 15 x HV (high velocity) shots fired at a mobile in the Turf Lodge. 3 x 7.62 returned. No CAS (casualties) NHC (no hits claimed).

Met the advance party at the docks. They had an Int brief and turned in knackered.

I went to Tac HQ, Springfield Rd RUC station. All very luxurious, but not much to do.

Phoned home.

Sunday 28th November

My NCOs went out on patrol with the Light Infantry. I went out at 1730 to monitor a torchlight procession demonstrating for political status for prisoners. All very boring and cold. We heard that as the procession moved up the Falls Rd a woman started streaking... horrible.

Soldier wounded in Londonderry, NSI (not seriously injured).

Civvies killed in Lurgan (Philomena Green) and Londonderry (Frank McConnellogue) by PIRA booby traps aimed at SF (security forces). PIRA admitted responsibility. SFNI (security forces not involved).

Monday 29th November

Mostly personal admin. Cpls Robinson and Blowers went out on the search at 0400. One black beret and syringe found, occupier lifted.

Went for recce of telephone exchange, our responsibility.

Organised a trip down the sewers for Wednesday, took over confidential documents.

Tuesday 30th November

OUR FIRST CASUALTY.

Had a drive around the Bn area to see the other Company locations, we've certainly got the best by far. We travelled in two open Land Rovers with a Pig and got pinged on the Falls/Springfield junction.

Yobs let loose with some rocks and one smashed the windscreen sounding like an LV (low velocity) shot…panic! The other hit L/Cpl Gibbins on the cheek. He was OK, just bruised but there was a continual flow of abuse from him for quite some time. The craphat officer i/c wouldn't stop despite our protests so we lost the yobs but we have a good description and there are four months to go!

One woman (Elizabeth Luney) shot dead by the UDA in Silverstream Rd, Ballysillan, our old stomping ground last year.

Wednesday 1st December

The first chalk of the main body arrived by air at about 1000 and having paraded at 0100 they are a bit knackered.

Sewer Patrol. Cpl Robinson and L/Cpl Gibbins dressed up in Peter Storm jackets and waders and went to investigate the sewers running under the mill. Eventually we managed to lift up a manhole cover and the smell that came up was rather unpleasant. Cpl Robinson went down and had a look and there was a nasty flowing stream of sludge so I decided that it would need the RE search team to do it properly mainly because of the danger of being overcome by fumes. When we got back no one would talk to us, being called amongst other things Willard and King Rat.

The first snow of the year fell today, luckily not very much but it is very cold.

OUR FIRST CONTACT

During the late afternoon Landrovers and a Pig were going up the Whiterock Rd from the Falls Rd in that order. Sgt Evans and his NCOs were in the Rovers with a craphat officer, the Pig was full of craphats. As they were approaching Macrory Park Sgt Evans heard a bang, he stopped his Rover and jumped out. Just then there was another bang and a flash on top of the Pig and a lump of the Pig went spinning across the road towards him. What happened was that an RPG-7 had been fired at the rear doors of the Pig but had gone over the top and hit the turret ring which was blown off. The driver and commander of the Pig were both shaken but OK. Had it gone a few inches lower it would have killed most if not all in the Pig. Follow up NTR. A lucky escape, apparently the rocket was fired from within a crowd on the Falls/Whiterock junction.

L/Cpl Emberson recalls:

Cpl Dave 'Rooster' Barber was in the Pig and later showed everyone how a piece of shrapnel had severed the laces on one of his boots – Ian Blonk Bland vehemently believed the severed laces were the result more of a 'flying clasp knife' post attack than any enemy action.

Night patrol pub visits – lots of angry glares but not much else.
One elderly woman SI (seriously injured) after being hit by a taxi on the Falls Rd.
Did my first stag of the tour 0130 - 0730 in the Ops Room, absolutely nothing happened.

Thursday 2nd December. The Battalion's Seventh Tour Begins.

0900 D Coy assumes command of TAOR (Tactical Area of Responsibility). Main body arrives am. one section to telephone exchange, remainder guard duties for NHS. Snow.
Finished duty in the ops room at 0730, had breakfast, went to bed, got up, had lunch and did a bit of personal admin. Such is the life of a subaltern.
On watch 1800-2130. Nothing happened.
Fhiona, my wife, phoned to say that she's going to the CO's wife's house for dinner.
Sgt Edwards arrested someone for assault… that'll cause trouble.
Despite all orders to the contrary the CO was seen wearing cam cream.

Shots fired by the Holy Cross Church, Ardoyne, SFNI.

Friday 3rd December

On watch 0730-1230. Nothing happened. Very heavy mist and frost. Traffic warden killed and bomb in supermarket, both Belfast, SFNI. 1915 just going to bed when there was a bloody great bang. General panic, much running about and extraction of fingers. It sounded quite close. It turned out to be a bomb planted by the OP in Old Park Road. Some damage to buildings, will get full report on Sat. OP and houses badly damaged, no casualties.

Saturday 4th December

On watch 0130-0730.

0445 – I tasked Cpl Young to assist a Jock patrol. The Jocks met a hysterical civvy who said that some people in the Long Bar (139 Shankhill Rd) had threatened him with pistols.

Cordon and search initiated, assisted by RUC. Initial find 1 x 9mm pistol. In the house 4 training pamphlets and one magazine of three rounds. Three pers arrested by RUC.

I then tasked the company search team to go up and dig out the bar completely. The search started at about 0615.

Total finds:

2 x 9mm automatic pistols.

1 x Luger.

1 x revolver, poss .38.

1 x Colt revolver.

1 x Martini Henry .22 target rifle.

1 x homemade Sten gun.

1 x not known (NK) magazine with three rounds of ammo.

1 x rifle cleaning kit.

17 x .32 rounds.

25 x .38 rounds.

25 x NK rounds.

25 x 9mm short rounds.

2 x silencers.

1 x SMG mag and ammo.

1 x .303 drill round.

28 x 5.56 rounds.

1 x Armalite mag.

1 x SLR mag with 20 rounds 7.62.

20 x .22 empties.

A couple of UVF posters.

Not bad considering it was outside our area. It shows what can be done by getting stuck in early. We are now not very popular in the Shankhill.

One of the people arrested was UVF chief 'Chuck' Berry.

L/Cpl Emberson recalls:

The 'civvy' was if I recall a Scandinavian (Norwegian?) seaman off a ship in the harbour – he'd been out drinking when he was invited back to the Long Bar and then jumped and robbed before escaping. Ah, that friendly Irish hospitality!

Anthony 'Chuck' Berry was possibly OC Belfast Bde UVF but certainly OC of the unit based on the Windsor Bar. The Long Bar was later heavily connected to the Shankhill Butcher (Lenny Murphy) and his team. I remember the RUC being quite sullen and resenting our presence and the full search – I got the impression that if we'd not been there a lot less would have been found!

Ref RPG attack on the 1st December the ammo was from an old batch which has been used before. This was the first RPG attack for about two years. Also it is now known that the rocket was fired from the back of a lorry which was then driven away.

0300-0400 Total of 10 x HV/LV shots fired at Support Company's sangar from Divismore Park. No cas, no fire returned. Several hits on their location. Sp Coy followed up and arrested two pers and found a couple of rifles.

Sunday 5th December. The old lady's birthday.

A very boring day to start with, very cold and frosty. I had a bash in the gym (air raid shelter) during the pm followed by a sauna which made me feel very much better.

Phoned home, all OK apart from Fhiona being rubber dicked for the wives club & visiting the Toms wives.

Two bombs in Londonderry, 200 and 100 lbs. both mixed with shrapnel. No cas but about ten buildings were damaged, also incendiaries used.

Went out on a mobile patrol from 2030-2359. Instead of being nice and frosty it was pissing down with rain, we came back in soaked through. Only a few people about not surprisingly since the pubs were shut as well.

We stopped a taxi to search it, the driver couldn't spell his name, wasn't sure of his birthday and didn't know what was going on except that he was going up to Silverstream in Ballysillan. I think that he was a genuine idiot poor chap.

Ref Support Coy's shootings on Sat/Sun they followed up and found a wallet containing a birth certificate and an address. Surprise, surprise at this address they found a man hiding and two rifles.

Monday 6th December

ATO (ammunition technical officer) defused a 25lb bomb mixed with shrapnel also a booby trapped .22 rifle set to go off if lifted. Both in Andy Town.

Our area is very quiet indeed.

Did a waste ground search am, NTR (nothing to report), also a lift and house search in Harrowgate St but the people to be lifted weren't there. However the search did produce some subversive documents and the occupier was arrested.

Tuesday 7th December

Slept in until lunch.

Out on mobile patrol 1400 – 1800. Pouring with rain, luckily we have the newly issued waterproofs, more about them later. Area very quiet, no incidents although women seem not to like having their bags etc. looked into, obviously it's not been done for some time.

Good news from DIFS (Department of Industrial and Forensic Science) – The Luger that we found on Saturday has been traced and is known to have committed fifteen, possibly seventeen murders! Anthony 'Chuck' Berry has confessed at Castlreagh (ve haff veys ov making you talk!) and more info and confessions are expected.

Kneecapping in Andersonstown.

Girl shot in the head in Mountainview, (Ballysillan) VSI (very seriously injured). Died 8/12. Named as Geraldine McKeown shot by NK Loyalist unit.

It is believed by Bn Int that PIRA are not prepared to risk a confrontation with 2 PARA, the area has never been so quiet, even the daily stonings have stopped. *(Author's note: don't talk too soon!)* Perhaps they are waiting for the New Year or Bloody Sunday anniversary or maybe they are waiting for us to make a balls up.

O-group for search of five houses in Oakman St Wed am.

Wednesday 8th December

Film 'Aces High' OK.

Out on patrol in the evening, all quiet.

Two bombs in the city centre, one in the warehouse of a man who wrote to the papers and said that the Army was ruining the economy of Belfast and that they should go! No cas.

Got a TV for the Mess at long last.

Brigadier of 39 Bde visited us, as usual the routine was completely messed up as everyone had to be there for the visit. Seemed like a nice chap!

Twenty two mortars found in Londonderry – lucky for some.

Thursday 9th December

On patrol 0900-1130. Frosty and sunny. Spotted a few D2 PIRA and Fianna (junior branch of IRA, runners and couriers). Some gave us false names and addresses, lifted them and dropped them off at Tac HQ for screening.

When Cpl Young found a pistol in the Long Bar on Saturday he saw a man in the window with a pistol drawn and was only just prevented by the RUC from killing him. On being told this the CO went rather white and was seen wandering off muttering things about the yellow card. Lesson: even COs should abide by cordon rules!

Had a gym/sauna session. On patrol in the evening NTR, just kids wandering about.

Our first press cuttings appeared today from the Irish News: *"The PARAs have been seen driving recklessly at night without lights showing and shouting abuse at young children and have been continually harassing ordinary people. Never an hour goes by without a patrol searching and asking ridiculous questions of people"* All very familiar stuff.

22 SAS have been given the go ahead to operate in the entire area of NI as opposed to just South Armagh. I should think that will scare a lot of people.

Friday 10ᵗʰ December

On patrol 0930-1200, very frosty, out with Cpl Robinson. Saw one or two baddies, the older locals are still quite friendly and willing to talk to all patrols. Otherwise all is still very quiet. What are they doing?
Film in the pm. Had a few NIRT students out with us.
A Lt in the UDR and his wife were blown about 100 ft (??) up in the air but escaped without serious injury. Shot heard by Cpl Barber at Falls/Springfield junction. NFTR.
A patrol from B Coy found the body of a man who had apparently died of natural causes.

Lieutenant Philip Russell from B Coy recounts the tale:

I was on patrol in Divis Flats one afternoon when I was stopped by a civilian who informed me that there was a dreadful smell coming from the flat next door to his, he added that he had not seen the elderly man who lived in that flat for some time. On arrival outside the flat, a small crowd of interested onlookers quickly gathered. I suspect they were neighbours who lived in flats on that same "spine" and, like most of the occupants of Divis Flats who were "on the Bru" (ie on the dole), were pleased of a distraction to their otherwise miserable lives. There was indeed a thoroughly unpleasant, sweet smell which was definitely not explosives so the situation needed to be investigated.

On arrival at the "spine", I posted a patrol at either end of the open landing to provide my team with cover in case the incident was a come on. In such a situation, there was a risk that the crowd would suddenly disappear and we would be left exposed to a "shoot" from somewhere overlooking our position. After knocking hard on the door and gaining no response, I kicked the door in and was almost overcome by the unmistakable, hideous smell of death. On investigation, I found the elderly resident dead in his bed, rigor mortis had welded his eyes open and the stiff body stared blankly at the ceiling. The rancid stink of a long dead man was truly awful, a woman appeared in the bedroom from nowhere, took one look at the body, started wailing - presumably because the deceased was a relative - and left the flat immediately. Neither she nor any of the onlookers wanted to enter the flat or do anything about the situation for which I can't really blame them ... I informed the B Coy Ops Officer Lt. David Benest who called an ambulance which, I presume arrived and took the body away ... the smell was nauseating so I made suitable noises of condolence and scarpered on more pressing business.

Divis Flats in the foreground.

Two women were stopped by us on Springfield Road and asked to open their coats and they refused. The arrival of a policewoman solved the problem.

Saturday 11th December

Two letters from home, that killed five hrs in the ops room!

A GPO van was hijacked on the Springfield Rd by two unidentified men and later found abandoned, undamaged by the Telex, possibly just used as a carrier.

A goodly write up in the Irish press today, the usual rubbish about beatings and harassment but this time we were called 'the merchants of war'. Hooray!

The driver of the GPO van found at the telex later turned up and said that they had been hijacked by gunmen. The van was cleared by ATO but apparently there was a strong smell of the infamous marzipan (co-op explosive) inside.

Portadown – fifty minor injuries when a bomb went off at a wedding reception, what a great way to start married life.

Londonderry – a soldier was shot dead by a sniper. Named as Sapper H. Edwards. RE.

Search team C/S 41A&D attached to A Coy task in Whiterock. NTR. Int says booby trapped finds are on the increase.

CQMS and L/Cpl Gibbins fighting for title of porn distributers. Gibbo was the victor.

I seem to remember the NIREP that came out the next day was headed 'A soldier was killed in Londonderry. It was a quiet day.' – I kept a copy of it for some time but don't seem to have it anymore.

A patrol from B Coy found a man who had been badly beaten up, he insisted his injuries were as the result of a car crash.

Sunday 12th December

On watch 0130-0730. Nothing happened.

In 'Visor' *(The weekly NI magazine for the Army)* the craphats had the cheek to claim that they made the find at the Long Bar last weekend. The article claimed that they found the first pistol and had entered the building. Both crap, they had cleared off before both incidents. The CO is fuming.

Slept all morning. Film, the Happy Hooker, rubbish.

The soldier recently shot in Londonderry was a sapper, the last man in a six man patrol and was hit in the back. It appears to have been a cowboy shooting rather than a snipe. We must reiterate the need for the last men in patrols to be alert 100%. That's what happened to the Fusilier who was killed just before we arrived.

About 160 Paddies went marching again in Clonard gardens with a band, the usual fiasco of walkabout followed by speeches. NTR. They were demanding political status for prisoners held in the Maze.

Bomb hoax at the Bostock nurses' home at the Royal Victoria Hospital. B Coy in attendance.

An old lady helped by one of our patrols after being mugged by the Children's Hospital on the Falls Rd.

Various reports of shots throughout the night.

Monday 13th December

A fairly chaotic afternoon. In Belfast there were about forty hijackings, six explosions, one civvy killed by gunfire and numerous hoaxes.

Our area was as usual quiet which seems to indicate that planning happens here. B Coy were kept fairly busy with hoaxes etc. A civvy was killed by yobs who broke into J W Halls brush factory in Wilson St. At 1215 two men both hooded and armed with revolvers burst into the factory and held up the staff and planted a bomb. As they fled they fired 2 x .45 shots at the factory staff. Roy Young, a meningitis victim, was hit in the head and died instantly. They fled in a stolen PO van. ATO was tasked and arrived at 1238 and the device was neutralised at 1530. A second suspect package was discovered but only contained dog food. Area declared safe at 1735.

Nick O'Connor (Code name Prophet. The Unit Press Officer) recalls:

On the cordon perimeter just after the factory bomb. Little fella waltzed up, adopted his 'I want to be in a picture pose', and then casually told me, "My da says I'm not to talk to you because all youse PARAs are a bunch of fuckin' shites."

When we went down to the factory with ATO and the RUC, the dog was sent in. When it came out it was licking its lips and wagging its tail with like 'egg yolk' all around its face. On its 'initial assessment' the dog had licked up most of the kid's brain fluid. The dog handler was not pleased, and the dog was quickly returned to barracks before the press could get a photo.

At the time we were told by the RUC that the boy had been executed (shot in the head) because he didn't comprehend what the baddies wanted. When Public Relations arrived from Lisburn they were keen to make a big splash about the IRA having executed a boy with an obvious mental condition. When I pointed out the dog's misdemeanour, and the possibility that the press might have got a photo of it, it was decided by those of a far higher pay grade, that we would not try and exploit the tragedy.

I have no recollection of the TV interview. Must have been drinking. Been drinking ever since (well, and for a long time before, if the truth be known).

There were a number of bangs throughout the night, mostly ATO's controlled explosions.

Saw Nick O'Connor on TV. Gym and sauna.

A Sp Coy patrol was stoned at Springfield/Whiterock junction by about 35 youths, one was arrested.

Tuesday 14th December

On watch 0130-0730.

A number of house searches were going on when I got up, presumably as a result of the bombings yesterday. One of the houses in Bombay St was full of NICRA (NI civil rights association) literature and posters, handkerchief drawings from the Maze. Although technically this is subversive we can't touch the owner even though they are known players.

Yesterday's bombings and hijackings were it seems all in aid of this political status for prisoners rubbish.

A Coy and Support Coy put in a cordon around the reservoir and culvert by the Whiterock Rd as a result of a report of two bombs on the dam. RE search team tasked and spent much of the day on the job. At about 1600 Sp Coy had a contact, 6-7 HV were fired at them from two different fire positions. One RE (Royal Engineer) was hit and taken to MPH (Musgrave Park Hospital) where he is SI. Results of the search not yet known.

A source gave a tip off that led to the searching of the Falls Taxi Association offices. The ground floor was searched, the upstairs was locked up. The key holder lives in Andersonstown, the craphats were asked to get hold of him, this they couldn't or wouldn't do so the search upstairs was called off. They decided not to force an entry in case it was booby trapped. The place was last searched in November when an Armalite was found.

On the way back from the search via the lower Shankhill Peter Akister found a Catholic from the Ardoyne who had been half strangled with wire and had been given a head job. He was still alive when the ambulance took him away to the RVH where he is VSI.

Ref Sp Coy shooting: The shots probably came from the south side of the graveyard, no firing point has been confirmed but Sp Coy did return 14 x 7.62. NHC (no hits claimed).

There were a number of bombings and hoaxes throughout the province.

We had a suspect car bomb outside Mackies foundry, ATO (Ammunition Technical Officer – Bomb Disposal) declared a hoax after blowing the car up. Poor old ATO has been running around like a blue arsed fly over the past two days!

Wednesday 15th December

Due to all the hijackings the powers that be have gone into state of mild hysteria. The standby now at times has to provide two full sections on the ground. This means people working eight on four off which is not going to be kept up for any length of time. As one wit said, 'We will probably come in from patrol to find the wog man on guard.'

Heard last night by a C/S talking to 4: 'You'd better hurry up with the ambulance, this guy hasn't got much longer to go.' The victim, shot in Aberdeen St yesterday was still very much alive at this time even though a lump of his head was missing, surely very reassured to hear this diagnosis. We are told Cpl Squires gets the prize for tact!

Heard on C/S 2's net: 'Bring the woman round here to me so she can see Felix (ATO) blow her car up.' (Maj. David Higginbottom, nice one.)

Worse than a head job? "The Army in Londonderry found a severed penis on waste ground. It was said to have been there for about two days. No one has been admitted to hospital to claim it."

B Coy had 6 x LV fired at the tail end Charlie of a foot patrol as it moved down an alley by Albert St. No cas FUNTR (follow up nothing to report).

An A Coy Pig crashed into a bus. A B Coy patrol arrested youths attempting to steal a bike!

Ref yesterday's search and contact: Two devices were found, each one full of 'shipyard confetti' connected to a command det wire. 10 lbs and 7 lbs each. On being shot at the three sappers froze, two were pulled down by Sp Coy and one stopped a bullet in the chest.

On patrol 2115-2315, all quiet. Shots heard in Turf Lodge. I went out with Standby 2 in a pig and rover. C/S 3 at 219 Springfield Rd reckoned that there were some people spying on them. We went down Springfield Rd and saw four yobs lurking in a corner. On being P checked one turned out to be PIRA and so just for good measure we lifted them and took them to Tac for screening.

Endless RAT TRAP after RAT TRAP calls.

Thursday 16th December

On watch 0730-1230.

Coy is now doing static guards on the Springfield Rd Post Office due to the extra cash being passed around prior to Christmas.

L/Cpl Gibbins' vehicle was involved in a minor accident, the Rover is OK but the civvy car is damaged.

Joy, five letters from Fhiona, all's well. Got one from Mum, the building has started, all well at home.

Sudden Flap: At about 2330 the CO arrived and had a word with Ben. Ben had an O Group. Apparently a source gave information that PIRA planned a day of bombings shootings and hoaxes, both against civvy targets and the SF. This would be tomorrow. The timings would from about 10-1700, the reason being the usual: 1000 gives them time to recover from the previous night and 1700 means that there is enough time for all the incidents to get on the 6 o'clock news! (A proven statistic). Bde detached 2 platoons plus Coy HQ from 1 Gordon Highlanders to us as a backup. During the O group Fhiona phoned to say she's going to stay with her folks.

One of our patrols found a debt collector who was complaining that he'd been robbed of £60.

Friday 17th December

DOOMSDAY??? No chance – area quiet as a mouse interrupted by the odd shot.

On patrol 0900-1130, 1345-1630, 0030-0215. Knackered.

Got a fairly fluent stream of abuse from a hog accusing me of harassment. She said that I was from the Whiterock base and would complain to the Major there. Fine I said, I wonder if she went to see OC A Coy. It started when she refused to give me her age so I said that I'll make a guess and put her at 50 ish. She was in her early 30's it appeared. Roars of laughter from the Toms.

During the day the Falls/Springfield were very busy with Christmas shoppers. Evening patrol was very quiet.

Saturday 18th December

Heard that Ro, my sister, was knocked down, phoned home and she's OK.

Good news: 1. Support Company shot three hijackers, one dead two injured. 2. Tour has been cut short by three weeks.

Bad news: At approx 1400 a soldier from A Coy was shot in the shoulder in the Beechmount area whilst on an admin run. 2 x HV fired and 18 x 7.62 returned at a suspected gunman in the window of 77 St James Road. NHC. A search patrol in the immediate area had one pistol round fired at them, they gave chase and fired 2 x 7.62 at the gunman as he climbed a fence into Celtic Park. One hit claimed. NFTR.

From 'Pegasus Magazine': *'It is ironic to think of someone as lucky when he has been shot, but Cpl Norman Porter (A Coy) was shot when a gunman opened fire at a patrol in St James Road is very fortunate. Although the Armalite round pierced his left hand and passed through his abdomen, he suffered no internal damage and was considered well enough to return to Aldershot for Christmas. In the follow up to the shooting a second patrol was also fired at. They returned fire, and think they hit the gunman.'*

Ref Cpl Porter see comments on 23rd February, all may not be as it seems!

On patrol 1230-1500.

We heard 1xHV in the area of Beechmount, probably that incident. The people of Beechmount are not very friendly.

Support Company shootings.

At about 1000 a car attempted to run down a sentry at C/S 5's location, at that moment a foot patrol appeared and the car tried for them. This was to prove a foolish move as the patrol blasted it. One died immediately, one a fifteen year old youth has hits in the head, chest and arm and is VSI. The other, a seventeen year old youth is also VSI with chest wounds. (Upon being searched the car revealed a shotgun and explosives – not true)

2025 1 x HV fired at RWF (Royal Welch Fusiliers) sangar, no cas.

Latest version of the shootings: A hijacked car attempted to run down a sentry and a patrol, one person in the car was seen to be pointing a pistol. 26 x 7.62 fired (blimey!) 1 x DOA, 1 x VSI, 1 x NSI. Nothing was found in the vehicle apart from a replica pistol. I was told that it was a flintlock.

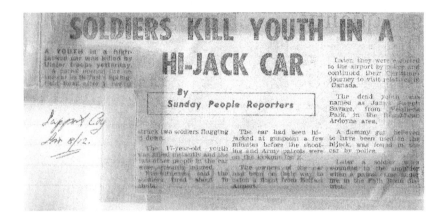

Sunday 19th December

A Catholic was shot through both knees and both elbows during the night in A/Town. SFNI, another punishment job.

During the follow up to A Coy's shooting a further NK number of rounds were fired at a foot patrol. Fire was returned and a man was seen to run off crying 'I'm hit, I'm hit!' No one has been admitted to hospital so he was probably treated by a PIRA doc.

On patrol 2030-2300. Pissing with rain all quiet but quite a bit of 'dicking' in the Clonard.

A car tried to run down Cpl Camp's patrol in Kashmir Rd. Lucky to be alive is the driver.

Phoned home.

Monday 20th December

On watch 0730-1230. Nothing happened.

B Coy reckoned they saw a man in a car with an MG. Rat trap, NTR.

Good press write ups over the w/e shootings. The Irish News accusing PARAs of 'grabbing civilians and holding them up in front of them to act as a shield against a hail of bullets'. Also 'Snipers gun down car' etc.

Had our third traffic accident of the tour, the second in 24 hours… no cas 1 x LR written off. Oops.

Tuesday 21st December

On watch 0130-0730. Only excitement was that a man threw his wife and four kids out of his house at four am!

Slept from 0800-1300. Letter from F.

On watch 1730-2130. Nothing happened.

A Coy had 1 x LV fired at them in Lenadoon Av. NFTR. Probably a low velocity backfire!

Visit of Lt. Gen. House.

Phoned home all well.

Wednesday 22nd December

On watch 0730-1230.

Funeral of John Savage (shot by Support Coy) down the Falls Rd, burial in Milltown Cemetery.

Explosion in University Rd near Sandy Row. Turned out to be as a result of a fire, probably a gas cylinder.

It has turned out that Savage and the two he was with were all wanted by the PIRA and OIRA punishment squads. It's now obvious why there was no reaction to the shooting. It would seem that they were freelancing.

8-9 x HV heard in Sp Coy area. NTR.

2134 contact in Sp Coy, 1 x HV fired at a foot patrol in Ballymurphy Cres. No cas.

Show in Albert St Mill. Didn't go luckily as it sounded rubbish apart from a black go-go dancer flashing herself.

Ref the explosion at University Rd, it was a car bomb and blew 1 x RUC to bits.

A man was battered to death in Forthriver Parade probably in a private dispute. Named as Thomas Easton, killed by the UVF.

A fifteen year old was shot in the bum in Cliftonville Rd. 2 X HV fired at Musgrave base, no cas.

Two teenagers were found kneecapped in Wilson St. Taken to RVH.

Thursday 23rd December

Lifted D. Quigley at 0630.

On watch 0130-0730.

B Coy dealt with two suspect cars both turned out to be hoaxes.

The usual round of hoaxes, assaults of soldiers etc. On the bright side Patrick Trainor was admitted to the RVH with gunshot wounds to his left knee. He was shot at home and it is thought that he might have accidentally shot himself.

PIRA unofficially announced a Christmas truce.

Phoned home, all well and cheerful.

Lieutenant Philip Russell recalls:

I was OC 4 Platoon, B Coy, based in Albert Street Mill, our TAOR covered the Lower Falls and Divis Flats, a particularly hard PIRA heartland. I recall the evening of 23 December well: it was freezing cold and it started to snow about the same time that the illegal drinking clubs in our area emptied and the drunks tottered back to their terrace houses in the Lower Falls and to their high rise flats in the Divis complex. Sometime after 23:00, it was reported that a hijacked car had been driven through one of the entry arches into Divis Flats and had been abandoned with all the doors open and the warning lights flashing. In response, and taking no chances that this might be a hoax, our OC (Major David Higginbottom) crashed everybody out (including the chefs, MT etc) to clear the Divis Flats complex. It was a massive task requiring far more troops than just B Coy but we cracked on as best we could leaving only the Duty Officer and signallers behind along with the "Chogey Wallah" and his 'Sexy Doreen' inflatable doll. I recall he had recovered her from a bin and she sported racy black masking tape that covered her many punctures.

Back to the clearance operation: there were not enough radios to go round so four man patrols (with radios) were posted at key points in the blocks of flats and they covered the physical evacuation operation. As the snow fell heavier, the night became colder and the occupants of the flats became more belligerent when we battered on their doors and ordered them to evacuate. Needless to say, the abuse was dreadful but we "helped" the unhelpful on their way and physically carried many old and frail people out of their flats, down the stairs and left them on the floor in the snow at the ICP (Incident Control Point) where, it was hoped, other occupants of Divis would help them.

My abiding memory of this truly awful event was arriving at the ICP with a shivering, elderly lady who I was hoping would stay alive until I could hand her over to someone else only to find a punch up had developed between a bunch of drunks and Pte "Woody" Wooding, the OC's bodyguard and a world class martial arts competitor. Apparently, some drunks had become abusive and threatening towards the OC and "Woody" decided to put them in their place and took them on single-handed doing a fine impersonation of Bert Kwouk of Pink Panther fame. The irony was that while the rifle platoons were trying to save lives and help the frail at the front end of the operation, "Woody" at Coy HQ was battering the civvies at the back end and making a pretty good job of it too!! It was certainly a Christmas to remember.

Christmas Eve

On watch 0730-1230.

Two people shot by troops in Dungannon. Both SI. An incendiary went off in Belfast and a couple in Enniskillen.

Lots of shoppers around, not much like Christmas here!

More on the University Rd bomb. It was traced by DIFS (department of industrial and forensic science) as almost certainly to have been made by C2 PIRA. The chemist is the hallmark of a training run by an ASU, new units apparently use chemists as targets whilst training. Why?

1 x HV fired at A Coy in Beechmount, no cas.

4 x HV heard in Springfield Rd.

Another kneecapping.

Suspicious car, batteries with wires on the back seat found. Declared false by ATO.

On patrol 2100-0100, mobile.

Lots of drunks and churchgoers. We received one Happy Christmas and a fair amount of abuse. There were about six drunken youths hurling abuse and beer cans at us from the sanctuary of the steps of the Church of St Paul, what courage and religious fervour.

All Coys wishing each other a Happy Christmas over the net.

Had a celebration can of beer.

Christmas Day

Woke up to find a bag of presents, mostly sweeties and a card from the blokes. That was really kind of them.

My Basha. Christmas Day. Note grey bag of presents from the lads.

2 x LV heard in the Falls area. NTR.

One of our patrols gave cover during the early hours of the morning to the fire brigade attending a fire at the Falls Rd Taxi Association.

Usual jolly Christmassy jokes over the net.

Officers and SNCOs served the Toms lunch in the cook house, despite the gloom they all looked happy! This was the first time that 2 PARA had been on ops over Christmas since Bahrain in '66 so we were told. Not bad considering that this is the seventh tour.

A carol service was held pm which the Toms quite enjoyed despite my having to go and drag them in to the comments of 'Happy fucking Christmas to you too sir!' Officers and seniors had dinner in the Sgts mess at 2000. It was quite good considering. CSM presented a statuette of a PARA to Ben as a premature leaving present. There was enough booze to make it quite pleasant.

A stolen minivan avoided one of our VCPs, chased, caught and two arrested.

Phoned parents and Fhiona, all well, though not quite what it should be. My first Christmas away from home.

A very quiet day in the province.

L/Cpl Emberson recalls:

I remember going out on a morning patrol on Christmas Day with Don MacNaughton – we 'P' checked Billy McKee ex-OC Belfast Bde PIRA (and possibly then PAC - Provisional Army Council) who was on his way to see his granddaughter. As we returned to NH St – a small child threw a small stone at Don and he nearly 'lost it'.

Don was greatly liked and respected but also known as 'Nutty Don' and was characterised by walking around chuckling to himself about God knows what thoughts. He was of Canadian descent. The consensus of opinion was that he'd gone slowly mad whilst being held for months under virtual close arrest on HMS Maidstone while his court case for attempted murder/manslaughter went through from the '73 tour.

He apparently became quite bizarre after he left the Army and lived reclusively in Aldershot before being 'discovered' quietly tending graves (over a period of years) in the military cemetery. He appeared in the news after being 'milk-shaked' on European election day while campaigning for The Brexit Party.

When he 'lost it' on the Christmas Day patrol it was quite spectacular – he pointed his rifle at the kid and then thought better of it and proceeded to throw his rifle, then his beret, then his flak jacket on the ground shouting words to the effect, 'that's it, I've had enough'. Nothing was said by any of us because of the respect and affection he was held in. I guess we'd call it PTSD nowadays.

'Windy' Blowers was also a bit 'postcards from the edge' at times – a placid, nice guy – very slow to anger – but when he did flip he flipped big time and it was a sight to behold!

Sunday 26th December

Phoned Aunt Alice & Co.

Dull. Nothing at all happened in the morning.

Ref Sp Coy's shooting, one of those classed as SI had his arm removed and will never be the same again. PIRA have not reacted to this incident at all which indicates that they couldn't care less about it. PIRA have failed in their promise to get a PARA before Christmas...

speak too soon and all that.

Nothing happened during the afternoon.

On patrol 1930-2130. Checked out a group by the Kashmir Wine Bar. They came from all the bad places in Belfast, obviously some meetings. A stolen vehicle crashed L/Cpl Camp's VCP, the next one gets a BR (Baton Round) through the windscreen.

Monday 27th December

Cpl Blowers found a fiver in Tralee St!

Explosion from RVH area during the early pm, it turned out to be a bursting tyre of a double decker bus, quite a bang.

4 x HV heard in the direction of Falls/Grosvenor Rd.

Pte McAteer left us, he volunteered to do a clerk's course thinking he'd be sent home, unfortunately for him it was held at Tac HQ.

On patrol 2030-2230. Did pub visits, the usual bad faces. NTR.

Caught some kids who were stoning up at Forthriver/Springfield. They shat themselves as we charged out of an alley and grabbed them. When I said we'd take them home and tell their parents one started blubbing.

On Cavendish St I saw a burning fuze about to be thrown, I cocked my rifle and was just about to fire when a kid of about 6-8 appeared holding a spluttering firework. I assured him that he was very nearly shot and he was suitably scared, as was I.

Phoned home.

Tuesday 28th December

0630 Lifted Tahill of Bombay St.

0815-1030 search.

A man, Paul Kerr, shot by the army in Dungannon has died. An enquiry is being held to find why fire was opened. More heads for the chopping block.

Spent from 0815-1020 frozen to the marrow doing cordon commander for the search. The area being searched was the waste ground around the stream at the Lower Flush. This ground is enclosed by high walls one of which forms the eastern side of Bomb Alley.

During the search a hurling stick, two children's homemade bows and a toy pistol were found. Fucking waste of time. Some time ago a bomb had been placed in the culvert but PIRA had removed it before firing. Don't know why, perhaps they thought there'd be too much damage to local property. It would have had to consist of several hundred pounds to affect anyone passing over. Maybe they thought the effort wasn't worth the possible result, who knows.

The lift went off OK, just for routine screening.

Two x 10-15lb bombs went off in the city centre, no cas.

On patrol 2130-2359, very cold and also very quiet.

Wednesday 29th December

Woke up to a stinking cold.

Pln on guard for the next three days so may get a chance to clear up my snot. Still below freezing outside.

On watch 1730-2130. Nothing happened except that the alarm in the cash and carry went off twice. NFTR.

Wagtail (sniffer dog) tasked after a patrol thought they smelt explosives. NTR.

1 x HV fired at Monagh sangar.

1 x LV fired at RUC.

1 x 7.62 fired by a soldier in a cordon in the city centre, 1 hit claimed.

A bomb planted in the chemists on the Antrim Rd was removed by a civvy then it exploded. No cas.

All quiet.

Thursday 30th December

On watch 0730-1230.

Put in for an early call at 0645 and got it at 0345. A good start!

No 168 Falls Rd was broken into by pers unknown.

Search of Beechmount community centre was NTR.

3 x HV fired at Royal Welch Fusiliers, no cas, no hits claimed.

Latest Int forecast (usually bollocks) (*"Thanks Dave," says Mike Emberson!*) is that most of the planning of operations is or will be carried out in the Coy or Bn area. This would include the construction of bombs and storing of weapons and explosives. It has been put to us to continue to increase VCP and spot checks on pers. Likely PIRA targets continue to be soft targets i.e. in the city centre and RUC, only attacking the Army for a specific reason or if a unit is becoming slack and presents an easy target.

Friday 31st December. New Year's Eve.

On watch 0130-0730.

Catherine Callaghan lifted for routine screening, nothing else happened.

During the morning a 10 lb bomb went off in the offices of the housing executive in the city, another smaller one went off in a shop. No cas.

Slept in till 1400.

On watch again 1730-2130.

A few more shots were fired at the craphats, no cas. A Coy found a .45 Webley pistol in Shield St.

A car blew up at 1930 in the Markets area, Joy St/Russell St junction. A woman was quite badly torn up. It could have been an own goal or more likely Prot retaliation for an incident that occurred last week when the Cats had a go at a Prot club in Alliance Av. Just off the Ardoyne.

A blast bomb was thrown at a craphat patrol in Andersonstown.

Ref car bomb, it was initiated when the woman turned on the ignition, she lost both legs and is VSI.

Saturday 1st January 1977

Did a recce for the route blocking op this afternoon. Whilst looking at the back of Hastings St RUC someone fired a shot, LV. It was quite close to us but I don't know who was firing at who, nobody seemed very interested.

The PSF organised a march from the Andersonstown up to the city centre in aid of the dreaded political status business. We were tasked to assist B Coy in blocking off the road by Hastings St RUC station. The road was blocked by a pig with another hidden (!) in reserve. The march went down the Falls without any incident. There were only about 350 marchers, a very poor turnout considering that there were about 6-10 organisations represented. The march was turned around at Divis St/Castle St junction and eventually dispersed without incident.

Bomb in Glengormley, 15 month old child, Graeme Dougan, was killed and parents VSI. Well done lads!

1 RWF opened fire following a contact.

A youth lost an arm in a booby trapped motorcycle.

Sunday 2nd January

On watch 0730-1230.

Five bursts of machine gun fire heard by C/S 42c in the area to our NE. Confirmed by Gordon Highlanders.

One soldier, L/Cpl D. Hind, Royal Highland Fusiliers, KIA and two injured in the market place in Crossmaglen. Paddy Devlin accused The Parachute Regiment of beating up and arresting people, then when they complained were beaten up again!

Search in Shankhill revealed one air pistol, 2 x .45 rounds, broken pistol grip.

A & Sp Coys reckon that their players are preparing for a snipe i.e. light signals, windows open and increased dicking.

The Q car crews also believe they are being followed.

Two sources have said that they believe that PIRA plan an offensive to take place from 3-7 January. Their targets will be predictably enough SF & RUC, bombings, kidnappings, assassinations etc.

Pte. Honer was seen in civvies on the Springfield Rd by Cpl Squires. He was attached to HQNI and was later reported as AWOL. He is now classified as lift on sight.

On patrol 2200-2359. Very frosty, nothing happened.

Monday 3rd January

At 0200 C/S 41F chased a man with a 'long thing' down Leoville St. They ordered him to stop and cocked their weapons but he managed to escape over a wall and disappeared. Bugger!

A number of bombs went off throughout the province, more being defused by ATO.

An AAC chopper crashed into a river in the country after hitting power lines. The pilot escaped but a crewman, possibly Sgt. MP Unsworth, Royal Hampshires, died.

At 1640 a D Coy patrol questioned James Clarke of 50 Forrest St just inside the gates of the Royal Victoria Hospital but he refused to identify himself. When the hospital security guards arrived they claimed that the patrol had no right to be in the hospital grounds and threatened to go on strike. When Clarke eventually identified himself he was allowed to go. Later his mother complained to the RUC that her son had been harassed but her allegations were so vague that further investigation is considered unlikely.

The incident was reported in the Irish News and the Daily Mirror. The reporting was factually incorrect in that no member of the hospital security staff was assaulted by the patrol and no complaint of such action was made to the RUC. Furthermore, the domestic staff and porters were not involved and did not threaten to strike.

On patrol 2130-2330. Area full of the usual boozers but otherwise quiet. More radio trouble. There is a big problem with radios in our area, not only are they going u/s but there are a number of bad dead spots in the Cavendish area. I had to come in due to u/s set. We have had to call in using red phone boxes occasionally. Tried to reverse the charges once, whoever was on the ops desk refused to accept it.

A bomb went off in Newtonards, no cas.

The CO reported a strange smell in North Howard St. Patrols did some sniffing but smelt nothing.

Tuesday 4th January

0600 two house searches, NTR.

L/Cpl Camp picked up a stolen car with driver Alex Tulley of 95 Beechmount Pass. He was taken to Springfield Rd RUC and charged. Name NK but he's not PIRA just a petty criminal.

On patrol 1230-1430. Very dull and trying to rain. Area fairly busy. We went to the Sinn Fein centre to buy a calendar.

A garage was wrecked in an explosion on the Crumlin Rd/Tenant St junct. Two explosions in Dunmurray, no cas.

1 x HV fired in Springfield area. NTR.

The telephone exchange had to be evacuated due a device in the NI Carriers premises next door. Declared a hoax.

A car was hijacked on the Falls/Springfield junction. The driver was taken into Walsh's Bar where he was forced to hand over his keys and licence. He was told to wait in the bar. Two hours later the hijackers returned and returned his keys and licence saying that the car was to be used as a bomb and not to tell the SF anything until later. This was eventually reported about four hours after the incident happened. No bombs have yet to be found. Phoned F.

Wednesday 5th January

PARAs made headlines in the Irish News, rather bad from our point of view. A certain soldier was accused of swearing and hitting two people with his rifle butt. It was naturally blown out of all proportion but does not look very good. The soldier in question is without doubt Cpl Young who is becoming a bit of a nuisance – for all our sakes he should be taken off the streets.

On patrol 0830-1100.

At 1040 Joe Morella of Bombay St stopped us and said that there was a suspicious object in his back yard. I took a look at it. It was about the size of a bag of sugar, wrapped in polythene and sellotape with wires sticking out. It had been thrown over the wall either from the alley or the derelicts in Cupar St. I tasked ATO and we set about clearing the houses nearby which went very well as the locals were keen to get clear and knew nothing about it. ATO arrived and declared it a hoax at 1115. It consisted of a lump of putty wrapped in polythene with two U2 batteries and some wires. It was obviously designed to intimidate the Catholics or to test our procedures or even act as a 'come along'. We returned without further incident.

4-5 HV fired at the RWF in Turf Lodge, 2 x SF cas both VSI. Two gunmen caught, one injured NSI. 1 x Armalite, 1 x sporting rifle, 1 x pistol found in the follow up.

The UVF claimed that their year old ceasefire is over, they also claimed responsibility for some of the bombs and hoaxes yesterday.

On patrol 2030-2300. We were ordered to lurk in the area of Forthriver Gardens to prevent the almost daily stoning that goes on. We spent an hour or so in the alleys but although there were plenty of yobs about they didn't do any stoning, not surprised really.

Went to Tac HQ for statements about the arrest of the man found with the stolen vehicle. The RUC tried on all the usual business i.e. 'we can't find the original statement, how about another?' Or 'it would make things easier for us if you just signed these blank statements.' And the favourite of all 'It's OK you can tell me, you did hit him didn't you? Don't worry it's just between you and me.' They must think that we were born yesterday. Soldiers have landed themselves in a lot of trouble by agreeing to such questions. Who's side are they on I wonder? A question that they ask us when we refuse to answer or agree to their proposals.

Thursday 6th January

Acted as cordon commander for the search of the SP Betting Shop in 24 Kashmir Rd. The search was NTR. I did find some anti Army literature in a pile of rubbish in an alley behind the shop, just the usual accusations of harassment.

Explosion heard in the north of the city, NFTR.

A 10-15 lb bomb was defused by ATO in the University area.

A bus was hijacked by 10-15 youths all armed with pistols according to the driver by the Monagh roundabout and later set on fire. The craphats seem to have lost control! It seems that their SOP is to patrol with pigs following them.

Friday 7th January

On watch 0730-1230.

Bomb hoax at Wellman's in First St. Anon male caller gave them ten mins to clear out which they did. After about half an hour it was declared a false alarm, they had one yesterday too.

Phone call from MoD saying that I've been given an extra year's seniority, date of commissioning has been backdated to 11th February 1973. Backdated pay too!

2130 I heard about 8-12 LV followed by 3 x HV. It turned out that the RWF were getting shot up again. About ten mins later a further 5 x HV were fired at them. No cas FUNTR.

On watch 0130-0730.
0235 Cpl Young arrested a pers for attempting to break into a car on Oranmore St. Two were local, one from Divis and one from Whiterock. All were traced as PIRA.
1 x HV fired at 32 Light Regt. RA in the Bone. Various shots fired at Monagh, no cas.
Search of the north part of the Flush revealed a bag of NK crystals – taken to DIFS, otherwise NTR.

Saturday 8th January. An ankle and thumb day.

1910 a large bang heard near this location. It turned out to be an explosion at Blackstaffs Bar on the junction of Springfield/Oranmore St. Two pers taken to hospital, condition NK. First thoughts are that it's an own goal or a bomb placed in the alley to the rear of the pub. A rust coloured Cortina was seen driving away but there is no trace on this.
2040 Suspect car bomb found on the Falls/Cupar St junction. As we are also finishing off with the Blackstaffs bomb things got a bit chaotic – cordons and road blocks springing up all over the place.
Heard on the net from C/S 43B (Cpl Barber) 'Send Starlight at your convenience, I think I've broken my fucking ankle'. He had too!
"The case of the missing thumb."
Suspect car bomb was at Conway St/Falls. ATO was tasked and declared it a false alarm. It turned out that this car was stolen. After it had been cleared by ATO RUC was tasked to take it away but meanwhile someone slipped into it and stole it again! A few minutes later it was discovered, crashed, just by Northumberland St. Inside it was found a fresh human thumb.
A few minutes later a B Coy patrol picked up a twelve year old youth running about minus a thumb and took him to RVH. Not really his day.

Sunday 9th January

On watch 0100-0730. Nothing at all happened.

A Felix, Sgt ME Walsh RAOC, was killed in county Fermanagh whilst he was dealing with a suspect milk churn. PIRA claimed responsibility. The tip off came by phone to the BBC.

A blast bomb was thrown at 2RWF mobile, no cas.

The two RWF shot on the 5th Jan are OK.

Ref the Blackstaff's bomb: It is now though that this was made locally and was left behind the pub to await collection. Why it went off prematurely is not known. If the Prots had tried to blow the bar up they would most likely have put it into the bar and not left it in the alley. Also they would not really want to start off the usual tit for tat runs again. The same goes for OIRA, why should they start up the feud again. The bomb consisted of 1-5 lbs of homemade in a gas cylinder. Rather a blow to C2 PIRA – especially to the morale of the carriers who must lose confidence in the bomb makers.

A cricket ball bomb was thrown at Monagh but failed to go off. Howzat?

The craphat who captured two gunmen and an Armalite on 5th January did so on his own. He challenged them to halt, cocked his weapon which promptly fell to pieces! The gunmen must have been caught as they were rolling about on the floor laughing.

Catherine Callaghan and Kevin Moyner arrested the other day by Cpl Bland for carrying a gallon of petrol and rags are now confirmed as having been interrupted whilst on a bombing run. Well done Blonk!

Cpl Blowers arrested the two yobs who stole the car that was treated as a bomb last night.

Orders for the searching of four houses tomorrow at 0500. Another hot tip from the Special Branch. The objective is to arrest certain people under the cover of a search which is a secondary task.

Cpl Blowers & Pte Smith…RUC want to see you here tonight. Get your story right!

Monday 10th January

On watch 0130-0730.

Search of the four houses at 0530, four pers arrested but nothing found.

Support Coy found six weapons, .22 rifles, a shotgun and ammo, as a result of a tipoff.

A woman living on her own at 23 Waterville St has been threatened several times by two NK males. She has said that if she places an ornament in her front window then she needs to speak to an Int patrol. These intimidations have apparently been trying to get a family to move in with her or better still to kick her out altogether.

L/Cpl Sullivan was hit by a stone thrown by a ten year old, he was lifted and handed to the RUC at Springfield Rd but later released. A quiet day.

Tuesday 11th January

On patrol 0900-1300.

Very heavy snow, the first of the year. Spent the patrol either shopping for Sgt Evans on the Shankhill Rd or doing VCPs. The only incident was that a snowball containing glass hit a driver on a VCP, not injured.

Cpl Robinson let the side down by dropping his magazine on the Springfield Rd!

All the snow was gone by the afternoon.

During the afternoon a soldier, Gunner E Muller RA, was shot in the neck at the junction of Old Park Rd and Mayfair St, he later died in hospital.

Graham Benton of 49th Field Regiment Royal Artillery recalls this:

I was a section commander with 49th Field Regiment, Royal Artillery in the

Markets area at more or less the same time so I was interested to read what it was like in other areas. You had a far busier time than us! Regarding Gunner Muller, having mustered from Junior Leaders he was posted to 49th Field Regiment while we were in NI so bided his time on rear party until he turned 18 years old.

He flew out the next day and in accordance with policy at the time he first had to go to Ballykinler for a week's training and then on the last day he was sent to another unit for evaluation / assessment by the relevant section commander he was put with, in this case a section of 12 Battery, 32nd Regiment Royal Artillery.

The story we heard was that he was out on a foot patrol in the Old Park Area and it was his turn as Tail End Charlie when he got shot. A memorial service was held at the Grand Central Hotel but the horrible thing was no-one in the Regiment actually knew him. Had he not been killed he would have joined us the next day. 32 Regiment only had eight days to go, 49 Regiment left early March.

A bomb destroyed a wallpaper shop on the Crumlin Rd.

Lieutenant Simon Barry of 3 PARA, my mate, was awarded a Mention in Despatches for work on the border.

A Mackies factory security guard said to one of our patrols to keep your heads down on Wednesday lads. Someone else approached and said they could say no more. We'll see what tomorrow brings.

L/Cpl Camp arrested two youths for stealing lead from the roof of Mackies.

A Coy are in orbit because they are convinced that they are going to be shot at from the Beechmount sometime this week.

Three shots heard in Sp Coy's area as an RIC (reconnaissance, usually a De Havilland Beaver aircraft) flight was going overhead, no one reported being shot at so presumably they were having a go at the aircraft.

Wednesday 12th January

Just read in today's NIREP that the RA had 1x HV fired at them on the Old Park Road on Monday that missed. The PIRA must have rezeroed their weapon, tried again and had a kill. A shame the RA didn't learn from the first shot.

On patrol 0500-0900.

Successfully completed a lift at 0630 without any problem although the wife rushed down to Springfield Rd RUC to give them a fairly good ear bashing. The Int took us to the wrong house at first so we just left a rather bewildered family rubbing their eyes as we walked out.

Went to the RVH to pick up some evidence, 2 x .23 rounds and an empty case recovered from the knee of a youth shot last night. The first round went into his knee, the empty case fell into the wound and the second round hit the empty case pushing it right into the leg! They looked quite juicy in a bottle.

Heard a series of LV shots getting closer, turned out to be a pig with engine problems.

A search of 125 Beechmount Grove. We were called upon to assist in the removal of in excess of 40 broken TV sets. The house was previously searched in October '75 when a large quantity of explosives was found. The owner was away, having jumped bail, and the house was occupied by two squatters. The TVs were all piled into two upstairs rooms. The supposition is that the bits and pieces from the TVs would have been used in bomb making. It took two four-ton journeys to remove them to the RUC dump for such things.

L/Cpl Emberson recalls:

I was on the TV search and asked for them to be removed – the father of the family at the address had a trace for bomb making and was OTR – the search was really to see if he was hiding at the house – I don't think having the TVs taken away was the most popular call by the Int ! But the family (wife and two teenage girls with attitude problems) seemed glad to see the back of them and reclaim their sitting room!

A bomb destroyed a house in Belfast and one in Londonderry.

Four bomb hoaxes at the ITS (Initial Towel Services) company depot in Sp Coys area.

PIRA admitted responsibility for shooting the gunner yesterday.

Snowed again and remains bitterly cold.

Thursday 13th January

0530-0730 Escorted R&R party to Aldergrove airport very cold indeed. One search was called off as no one was in, the other NTR.

On patrol 1530-1800. Area as normal. I found an electric motor for the timer from a street light dropped outside the SP betting shop. Handed to RUC.

A lion escaped from the circus and was seen wandering around the city. It was later caught by the RUC. A soldier died in the city when a wall blew over and buried him. Shit.

Sp Coy found a command detonated claymore device consisting of a galvanised iron bucket with 2-3 lbs of Co-op, 1 lb of frangex (Irish commercial gelignite) and a few lbs of confetti. The command wire and fuze was led out from the base of the bucket. The would be firing point was in a disused garage. It was found by Pte Robin Horsfall (Later SAS and of Iranian Embassy siege fame) who was lying down as a part of a cordon. He scraped away some earth and there it was.

See next photo.

L/Cpl Bell arrested a man for assault. It is understood that L/Cpl Bell was forced to defend himself!

170lbs of Co-op, dets and timers was found in the Markets area.

Friday 14th January

Search of waste ground, NTR. Snow, sleet and cold.

An RUC, James Greer, was killed in Co Antrim when his car exploded as a result of a PIRA booby trap.

45 x .45 rounds found by A Coy.

A small command det device exploded on the Crumlin Rd shop fronts just as a mobile went past. No cas, FUNTR.

A bomb destroyed a shop in the city centre, no cas.

A brown, plain package was delivered by mail to Mark Whitford – the customs label gave away the contents as being pharmaceutical articles. He wouldn't come clean!

Members of the ASUs from A, B & D Coys areas were seen together in the Clonard, no doubt an O group of sorts going on.

On patrol 2330-0100. Very heavy sleet and so the area was very quiet apart from a load of drunks staggering out of the Orient Bar on the corner of Cupar/Springfield.

Possibly 1 x LV not far from us on the Springfield not far from Blackstaffs. Went to investigate and no one knew or heard anything as usual.

At about 0045 there was what sounded like a good gun battle towards the Ardoyne, approx 20 x HV fired. This was shortly confirmed by the siren of an ambulance. No further details though C/S 0 said it was at the bottom of the Crumlin Rd.

Saturday 15th January

A search of the waste ground to the north of Mackies was NTR.

On patrol 2230-0030. Lots of Saturday night drunks.

L/Cpl Jones (Int) & L/Cpl Jones (43) had 1 x HV fired at them on the junction of Ainsworth Av and Shankhill Rd. FUNTR.

Witnessed a good brawl in a taxi by the Falls traffic lights. A young woman was battering quite a large man with her umbrella. At length everybody joined in and there were fists and boots flying. When it spread beyond the taxi we stepped in and kept the combatants apart.

An ambulance was tasked to take a woman from her house in Clonard Gardens. She had thrown a wobbler and was throwing the contents of her house into the street. Her neighbours said that it was a nervous breakdown and that they knew it was bound to happen one day what with the Troubles and all!

A soldier was shot in the leg in Strabane NSI.

5 x HV fired at a RWF patrol assisting RUC.

There were about four civvies involved in shootings, one lost his hands when a 5lb gas cylinder bomb went off.

The black taxis are threatening to block main roads due to Army harassment.

Sunday 16th January

Sp Coy found the half naked mutilated body of a woman in the Falls Rd cemetery. She had been tortured before being shot and killed by a bullet in the mouth. As a cordon was being set up to protect the RUC 5 shots were fired at it. No cas, no fire returned. It's not been attributed to any group.

An SAS patrol killed a gunman, Seamus Harvey PIRA, near the border by Crossmaglen. The gunman was wearing a mask and combat kit and was carrying a pump action shotgun. During the firefight two other gunmen opened fire, fire was returned and they fled leaving 2 x 5.56 empties. The s/g was loaded with heavy gauge shot suitable for deer etc. PIRA admitted that he was a member.

On watch 1730-2130.

A minor explosion in the city centre.

2 x HV fired at Sp Coy, 7 x 7.62 returned.

During a planned follow up the RWF recovered a loaded Armalite in Turf Lodge. The cordon was stoned and bottled by about 200 youths and 13 x BR were fired, 11 hits claimed.

Monday 17th January

On watch 0730-1230

0200 Cpl Young arrested two males for assault on SF. He was operating a snap VCP by 219 Springfield Rd. He stopped a car and the occupants – rather drunk – failed to cooperate fully. One of the Toms who was taking down particulars had difficulty in understanding the man. There followed a fairly fluent stream of abuse. One of the men attempted to assault Cpl Young and they were both promptly arrested. On the way to Tac HQ further trouble ensued in the Landrover. At Tac one of the civvies went berserk and took a swing at Cpl Young and connected with his eye. In the ensuing scuffle the civvy received a fractured skull, a broken collarbone and sundry bruises.

An A Coy sangar saw a gunman in the Whiterock area, Nitesun was tasked but was NTR.

Op Platypus was put into operation to try to pick up the elusive Garrand. A source said that two men would drive up outside the RVH and then it would be passed to two others. An ambush was laid on the junction of Cavendish/Falls Rd from 1845-2000. The ambush was to have been sprung by the IO who was lurking in civvies, long hair and with a pocketphone.

No one turned up so it was called off.

Someone set fire to a car by the peaceline by Ashmore St. It was just about burnt out by the time the fire brigade turned up.

On watch 1730-2130

A Coy called for our standby section to be stood to in case they needed assistance. They did not say why and eventually stood down.

Tuesday 18th January

On watch 0730-1230. The woman found dead the other day by Sp Coy was strangled as well. Search of two occupied houses and two lifts. One hypodermic syringe found.

The CID and Bomb Int have told us they are very pleased with the find of all the TV sets on the 12th. It is likely that some of the components were to have been used for bomb initiation.

When C/S 43B was sent to see a Mrs Ball of Clonard Gardens to ask her to see the RUC he was told to fuck off and had the door slammed in his face!

Cpl Young has got himself in the Irish papers again… Mad John. They say that Mr Moore received severe lacerations, fractured skull and numerous other injuries. It also says that the soldiers danced on Mr Moore after having beaten him to a pulp. Not very clever.

On watch 1230-2130 nothing happened.

Craphats had another contact. Several rounds fired at SF bases.

C/S 3 found a suspect package in the in the downstairs lavatory on Crumlin/Agnes St. Hoax.

1 x HV fired at a patrol in New Lodge. No cas, no fire returned.

Wednesday 19th January. Halfway through.

A number of police reservists have spotted booby traps fixed to their cars or houses. All safely defused.

SIB want to interview Cpl Johnson ref the report of the theft of a bottle of aftershave and a bottle of sherry from a house searched over two weeks ago. As the clearance chit was signed by the occupier of the house, a squatter, they are wasting their time.

The intimidation in Waterville St goes on. An eighty year old woman was told she had forty eight hours to get out of her house or else. The organisation responsible is the 'Clonard Housing Committee' a branch of PIRA. Their aim is to put certain families into a particular area. No alternative accommodation would be provided. When asked why she did not go and see the Fathers in the Monastery she said that it would be a waste of time as they are not interested in that sort of thing. Christians eh?

The chief priest at St Pauls refused to see the CO saying that ever since 1974 he had given up talking to the Army. This was in relation to accusations of Army harassment. The clergy here are all well off and quite safe but won't lift a finger to assist anyone else but themselves.

Found in 111 Beechmount Crescent 1 x BR empty case and projectile, souvenirs.

Two youths attempted to hijack a car in Cavendish St. The driver drove through them and stopped L/Cpl Bell and told him about it. The driver was very shaken indeed and was still trembling. The two resident RUC (Constables MacFarlane and Rush) were informed and they immediately jumped into their civvy car and drove around trying to get hijacked so they could shoot the hijacker or do a Kojak. Obviously both quite mad.

PIRA officially claimed responsibility for killing the gunner on 11th January, how considerate of them.

1 x HV fired at a foot patrol in New Lodge, no cas, 3 x 7.62 returned.

Thursday 20th January

Three bombs went off in the new Co-op building, damage not too bad. The building was constructed at a cost of £10 million and was due to be opened next month. The original Co-op was destroyed by a bomb in 1972.

A warning has been sent out saying all Co-ops and chemists are going to be targeted.

Craphats found an SLR with SUIT sight in the Ardoyne, it was lost some time ago by the Army.

A RWF base in Turf Lodge was mortared at about 2000, no cas.

On patrol 1300-1700.

We were tasked to search Co-ops and chemists for bombs, nothing found. Did a few more VCPs. Went to Carringtons to see the manager to update our records. Rain.

1 x HV fired at the front sangar of RUC Andersonstown. No cas, no fire returned.

A pamphlet entitled 'The construction and operation of booby traps' together with batteries, wire and capacitors was found in a workshop in the grounds of the Holy Cross Church.

Friday 21ˢᵗ January

Ref mortar attack, no rounds hit the camp but did hit a community centre. Several people were suffering from shock. Not very good publicity for PIRA as though they care.

'A reliable source' said that PIRA were going to have a go at the SF today from 1200 onwards and that it would start with the hijacking of some vehicles.

On patrol 1300-1700

One man carded as PIRA was shot dead by SF in Co Tyrone.

Six buses hijacked and burnt out in A Coy's area, one in the Ardoyne and the rest in Turf Lodge. Also one taxi burnt out. One man slightly injured.

A mortar base plate was found in a lorry about 150m from Monagh Camp, three rounds had exploded, two destroyed by Felix in situ, one missing in the mud probably.

A single NK round was found in the Falls cemetery, it was attached to a piece of fishing line attached to a 5lb anti personnel charge. Neutralised by Felix.

A prison officer escaped when he discovered that his car had been booby trapped by the Crumlin Road Gaol. ATO destroyed it in a controlled explosion.

There is a magic device due to be introduced to SF in March that instantly indicates the direction of the firer if the round comes within 5m of it. It is not man portable.

False alarms outside our base, as suspicious beer keg was found by C/S 42S at Connaught/Third St junction. Felix arrived and fired a shotgun cartridge at it and declared it a hoax.

Robbery on Springfield Rd at 2315, SFNI.

Saturday 22nd January

0800 area search by C/S 42 NTR.

Early lift at 0630 successful.

Soldier slightly injured when his Landrover set off a booby trap in Co Londonderry.

Young girl shot, NSI, in Newry in crossfire between RUC and gunmen.

Warning of another PIRA offensive…

RUC are to be equipped with M1 carbine to replace SLRs and SMGs.

A Coy find as a result of a tip off consisted of:

1 x .303 Lee Enfield No 4 rifle.
1 x 9mm Browning pistol.
90 x .303 rounds.
20 x 7.62 rounds.
12 x 9mm rounds.
28 x 5.56 rounds.
1 x SLR magazine.
1 x 9mm magazine.
2 x 5.56 magazines.
9 x electric detonators.
A quantity of cordtex.
Subversive literature of Int interest.

On patrol 1900-2130 nothing going on.

Someone has obviously gripped the locals about the state of the back alleys. During the 2-3 weeks after Christmas it was almost impossible to get down some of them because of the piles of junk and rubbish. Now they are fairly clean apart from dog and human turds carefully laid to catch out the unwary foot patrols.

A shitty Clonard alley.

A heavy smell of marzipan in Cavendish St, wagtail tasked but NTR. Probably explosives in transit rather than a permanent hide. Also a trace behind the Kashmir Wine Store.

1st Bn Devon and Dorsets (D&D) took over from 32 Light Reg Royal Artillery in the same area we had last year.

Kneecapping in New Lodge NSI.

Sunday 23rd January

Thought of the year from D Coy Int Section:

"If the nation trains a body of men to the standard of an elite fighting force, then that nation must expect those men to kill when provoked." Mike Emberson claims authorship!

A soldier from 3PARA was charged on Friday with the manslaughter of a girl killed in crossfire in Armagh last summer.

A soldier from the UDR was injured following an ND with a pistol in the city.

A car was found burning merrily in the Shankhill. When it was put out it was found to contain two crispy bodies. It has so far been impossible to identify even their sex let alone an identity. (Thomas Boston, John Lowther shot by NK Loyalist group.)

From Cpl Bob Powell Sp Coy:
"We plod the streets, we search the cars where terrorists are our prey, we sometimes work around the clock for 50p a day.
For those of you who find it hard to understand our crib
We'll take a closer look to see how we earn that half a quid.
We get 1p for a P check
2p for a find
1p for a VCP
Yet on and on we grind.
3p for an occupied search
a derelict we get two
5p for a contact
but now they're getting few.
1p for a sense of humour
2 for trouble and strife
10p just in case you don't
get back to see your wife.
3 is for the Copper's job
that we do every day.
3 to say how happy you are
when the bosses come to stay.
Now that concludes our total
I make that thirty three,

Oh yes 17p goes back in tax
To help pay our 50p."

Author's note May 2019: *From Hansard December 1977.*
The average industrial wage in this country is £76.80 a week. A private soldier gets £23 less than that. His weekly wage of £53.55 is two-thirds of the industrial average. If he is a married man with two children living in Army quarters, his takehome pay is £32.27 a week. Officers do not fare much better. An unmarried second lieutenant gets £60 a week—about £16 less than the average industrial wage-and his take-home pay is £33.38.

1313 a number of HV were fired at an RWF patrol, no cas, no fire returned.

Points from the Brigade & Battalion conference:

1. It is thought that the OIRA may start an offensive against the army and RUC.
2. On Tuesday 18th it is believed that an arms and explosives resupply was sent into the Whiterock to be distributed to PIRA subunits.
3. It is thought that there is a punishment squad provided by B2 PIRA who do all the kneecappings in 2 PARA's area.
4. D2 PIRA have been given a bit of a shakeup and that the chain of command has been altered. It is possible that they may become more active.
5. There is no indication that anything has been planned for the Bloody Sunday anniversary next weekend.
6. It is believed that the burning of buses is used to distract SF and act as a diversion.
7. It is possible that more mortar attacks are on the way. A patrol from RWF overheard a conversation just before last week's attack. They knew the target, type of attack, type of rounds to be fired and an approximate firing point. What they did not know was the time.

8. The reason for all the Co-op bombs was due entirely to bad security. Checks every morning consisted of lining up the workmen and saying 'Hands up all those who normally work here'. No wonder they got hit.

9. Nail bombs have been found and used in Turf Lodge.

Well that lot didn't tell us anything much!

On patrol 2100-2330.

Foggy, very few people about.

A soldier, Gnr G Muncaster RA, was killed instantly by a gunman in Eliza St, Markets at about 2200.

Graham Benton of 49 Field Regiment Royal Artillery recalls this:

Our other fatality was Gunner George Muncaster who was killed on 23/1/77 and was a good friend of mine. His section had just gone out and we'd just finished a 16 hour shift of footsies, mobiles and standby and I was just handing in my Pye set when the contact came in at 22.06.

Needless to say we were straight back out along with the standby section as it was only a few hundred yards away. Unfortunately there was nothing anyone could do to save him and I describe the events of the evening in one of Ken Wharton's books and its effect on me. Although the rifle used was recovered by our successors, the gunman was never identified or found.

The two bodies found in the burnt out car this morning had been killed by GSW before being burnt.

Someone stopped OC NITAT, Maj. Lindsay, he was lost!

Monday 24th January

A young man arrested by Cpl Robinson for throwing stones was laid out by Pte Fleming when he tried to take a swing at him.

A young woman arrived at B Coys location in labour. The B Coy medic took her to the Belfast City Hospital where she gave birth to a son.

Ambulance tasked by C/S 43L to take J. Quigley PIRA to hospital with a burst ulcer. I hope they went the long way round and over as many sleeping policemen as possible!

1450 – 1 x HV fired at a B Coy patrol on Falls Rd somewhere between Albert and Ross St. The round hit the swimming baths at North Howard St. This ambush may have been laid following the reshuffle of the command of D2 PIRA (Lower Falls). It was more than likely intended to hit one of our patrols entering or leaving NH St. No cas, no fire returned.

1830 – As a result of a routine car check we were ordered to search Nos. 33 & 39 Iris St. I was commanding this rather rushed job. Cpl Barber's search team in No 33 found a pile of documents of Int interest, 3 x 5.56 Armalite rifles in good condition and a fertiliser bag. Each rifle had a full magazine on. The other search was NTR. Shows the value of regular car and P-checks.

If I recall rightly a search dog (black Lab) was called to 33, searched the house, found nothing & then went to sleep on the sofa. As Rooster was about to leave he said we'd better have a look behind the settee, moved the dog off and found the guns. However that may be apocryphal embroidery.

See next photo.

On patrol 1330-1545 Area very quiet apart from the sniping.

A UDR soldier was shot in the stomach with a shotgun and is in hospital NSI.

RWF fired at from a passing car, no cas. 4 x 7.62 returned which hit the car NFTR.

There has been no immediate local reaction to the Iris St find.

Ref 39 Iris St, no one was in so a forced entry was made with a neighbour as a witness. The owner of the house was in hospital but his two sons who usually live there were out although their car was parked nearby.

Tuesday 25th January

0530 – two occupied searches found 2 x .45 empty cases, 2 x green berets plus a large quantity of subversive literature that included photos of SF.

One of the sons living at 39 Iris St gave himself up this morning, the other is lift on sight.

L/Cpl Bell was accused of assaulting a civvy at a VCP, who works for the NI Housing Executive. This is obviously completely fabricated and is just another smear campaign. Apparently.

Pte Dave Smith:

I remember Cpl Dinger Bell on a mobile patrol late at night, we stopped to question some bloke who took offence and told Dinger he was a hard man with a gun. Wrong move; the rifle sling came off his wrist, handed his weapon over to us and said, 'I haven't got a gun now.' End of conflict! Don't argue with Dinger.

Brigadier Geoff Howlett visited.

A human leg was found in the Divis Flats, given time we will be able to build a complete man with all the spare parts lying around.

Yesterday's find was confirmed as:

2 x AR15 Colt Armalites.
1 x AR18 Japanese Armalite.
1 x 30 round mag.
2 x 20 round mags.
20 x 5.56 rounds.

The weapons were hastily concealed therefore probably in transit.

An incendiary device was found in the Co-op on the Springfield Rd. Cpls Johnson & Doolan were sent to investigate. It turned out to be a Mk IV in a plastic carrier bag. The area was cleared and Felix tasked. As Felix was approaching it, it ignited causing moderate damage to the shop. When asked why he didn't try to put it out he said 'Oh all right, if you want' and wandered back to his Saracen to collect his extinguishers.

The device was planted by two youths wearing blue anoraks and hoods one of whom was armed. They made their escape in an unknown direction. It was not known who did it or why.

Ref L/Cpl Bell's alleged assault – Sinn Fein have gone mad and changed their story, this time it was four people assaulted and no mention of a car.

As a follow up action to the incendiary in the Co-op three houses were searched. One was empty and was cancelled, one was NTR and one called off. This was in Bombay St. After the search had been going on for about fifteen minutes the owner of the house Frank Moyner had a convulsion and said that he was having a heart attack. His wife had been going fairly berserk throughout the search and was threatening everyone with lawyers, MPs and death. Eventually Moyner keeled over and expired.

His wife refused to allow the soldiers to give any resuscitation or medical assistance and she threw Holy Water all over the place. Holy Paratroopers. The team left just as a priest arrived. On the news later it was said that PSF accused us of murder by refusing access to medical teams. And so the smears go on.

1 D&D was shot in the leg in New Lodge, NSI.

A shoe shop was blown up on the Crumlin Rd, no cas.

A house belonging to an RUC was booby trapped in Co. Londonderry, no serious cas.

The documents and tapes found in Iris St were described as being of very great importance, they have gone to SB and HQNI.

Cpl Young has been taken off the streets as a source said that he was on the PIRA death list. He turned up in the Ops Room not long ago for a patrol brief wearing desert wellies. He says they are more silent. I pointed out that the rest of his patrol have standard issue DMS boots on. I told him to go and get changed, he seemed a bit upset. He's actually a bit odd. Otherwise a quiet day.

The doctor who was called to the late lamented Moyner has refused to sign a death certificate which means an inquest. It could go rather badly for his wife.

L/Cpl Emberson:

I recall this well! It was Rooster's search team again. It was a well conducted 'by the book' search. The occupants were hostile from the start and Frank M who was in his late 60s wouldn't stop shouting and bawling. Eventually he went into what was obviously a heart attack and collapsed into a chair. Some pills were produced by the family and I placed one under his tongue to dissolve but it did little good. As I was then clearing his airway and asking for help to get him on the floor to begin CPR it turned into a bit of a brawl in the front room and a crowd gathered outside. Eventually Rooster called it, saying an ambulance was on its way and we extracted ourselves to a volley of bricks and spit. Some months later we were all called back for the inquest (with jury at Crumlin RD) and spent a few days on the cruise ship HMS Maidstone. At the inquest the doctor gave the post-mortem result which indicated a long history of heart problems and that upon examination his heart was 'twice the normal size' and expressed the opinion that he could have died at any time and it was surprising he had lived so long. The coroner gave clear directions but the jury (drawn from the Falls & Clonard) returned a verdict of unlawful killing. NFA was taken by the Army/RUC but no doubt at some stage I'll get a visit from PSNI's Historic Enquiries Team.

2/Lt Warwick Stacey recalls:

I remember telling Embo not to pump his chest, as I had been told that to do a good job on that you had to hear ribs crack. I didn't think that would be a good look at any subsequent inquest. I think Embo was wrong on the 'unlawful killing' return by the jury. It was a 'no verdict / no result' or similar. I was told by a lawyer that while that did not quite brand us as killers, it still left us smeared with assumed guilt.

HMS Maidstone. *A former submarine depot ship. She was used as accommodation for military in transit etc.*

My recollection:

I stayed in HMS Maidstone in 1972 when ashore from HMS Kellington (I was a Midshipman RN and gunnery officer in Kellington, a mine hunter) doing anti-gun-running patrols off the coast. It was here that I first heard a shot fired in anger by a paratrooper in Ballymurphy. We captured an ancient rifle from a trawler and whilst going ashore to some long forgotten harbour in a Gemini inflatable to hand it to the RUC one of the sailors managed to drop his SMG into the sea. What a laugh that was paperwork wise!

I was there again in 1975 when I was in court following the 'dust up' at Baden Powell St. We were accused of GBH – BRs fired and batons wielded. In the end we were not charged but Mr George Watters and some others got done for assault.

Wednesday 26th January

The expected reactions to yesterday's death have occurred: The threat that an Armalite would be used against us (2 sources). Whistle blowing and dustbin lid banging. News hysteria.

The news, TV and papers, predictably presented a one sided story mainly 'because the army wouldn't comment.' Someone in HQNI should have issued a statement giving the true story. They allege that medical assistance was refused, that the ambulance was delayed, that the man was assaulted, that his wife was assaulted and so on. The local MP Gerry Fitt has called for the withdrawal of The Parachute Regiment etc.

The truth of the matter was that Mrs Moyner was refused permission to leave the house twenty minutes before the death – normal search routine to keep the occupants inside. She was running all over the house, contrary to procedure, and her hysteria had a definite part in bringing on the attack. Once the heart attack took place she refused to allow any medical assistance to be given by L/Cpl Emberson. A doctor and priest were called immediately and the patrol withdrew once the priest arrived.

It is disgraceful that no official statement was released immediately. Ben Hodgson and Warwick Stacey should have been allowed to tell their side of the story. It has been announced that there will be an official enquiry into his death.

On watch 0130-0730. Very quiet.

DIFS has traced one of the Armalites to a shooting incident in Blackstaffs Bar in Nov '76 when 2 x 5.56 were fired at an RUC vehicle. No cas.

10 x HV fired at a D&D patrol, no cas.

A 7.62 rifle and several pistols, ammo, mortar parts and a target list and run routes were found in Andersonstown.

An eight year old boy was seriously injured when a booby trap exploded in Strabane. He bent down to pick something up and it went off. It was intended for SF, presumably the cat gut merchant again. A bomb exploded in Castle St damaging an OP, no cas.

WIVES IN 'TROOPS OUT' BID

FOUR housewives yesterday began a fight to remove paratroopers from their streets.

They asked other women in sign a petition against the crack troops.

The housewives warned, "We will present the petition to the Government.

"And if that doesn't work we will drive the paras out of the district ourselves."

The troops are operating in the Clonards area of Belfast.

The outcry began over the death of 65-year-old Mr. Frank Moyna, at his home in Bombay Street on Tuesday night.

Routine

He died of a heart attack while paratroopers were searching the house during a routine check on the area.

His family claimed that the soldiers stopped them sending for help.

And yesterday the police began an inquiry into the incident as SDLP politician Mr Paddy Devlin lodged a formal complaint.

Mr. Devlin has demanded the withdrawal of the paras from their Springfield Road base.

"The conduct of this regiment has caused nothing but trouble in the area. They are doing more harm than good," he said.

SDLP leader Mr. Gerry Fitt said: "I intend to raise this incident with Defence Secretary Fred Mulley, at the earliest opportunity. The conduct of troops in Ulster is his responsibility."

An Army spokesman said: "The soldiers involved were aware of Mr. Moyna's condition. As soon as he had a heart attack, they rushed for an ambulance and a doctor."

PAGE 9

Now the Paras face dustbin lid 'war'

By TED OLIVER

ANGRY housewives last night threatened to drive the crack Parachute Regiment out of a Belfast district.

The women of Clonard on the Falls Road claim soldiers refused to allow medical aid through to 93 - year - old resident Frank Moyna who died of a heart attack when the Army searched his home.

They say the Paras pulled his wife Mary back by the hair as she tried to call for help from a window, and that a man with first aid experience was refused entry to the house.

By the time local priest Father Peter Burns was allowed in Mr Moyna had died.

One of the women, Mrs Theresa Quigley, said: 'We will fight the Paras from street to street. We will use sticks and whistles and bin lids. We are not afraid of them.'

Wider

Mrs Kathleen Pohill added: 'We don't like the Army but we will put up with any regiment other than the paratroopers.'

Mr Moyna's death has already caused a wider protest against the regiment and Mr Paddy Devlin of the SDLP has made a formal complaint to the police.

The Provisional Sinn Fein are organising a 'Paras out' petition which will be given to Northern Ireland Secretary Mr Roy Mason.

Army officials said last night they could not comment while the police were investigating the incident.

Thursday 27th January

1 x HV fired at a sangar in the city centre, no cas, 2 x 7.62 returned, NHC.

On watch 0130-0730.

Someone broke into a disused warehouse on Third St/NH St junction, reported by the front sangar. Cpl Johnson and RUC went to investigate, NTR.

Very heavy fog during the night, vehicle patrols very difficult as viz was eight to ten feet. The usual daft radio messages!

A number of cars blocked the Clonard during the afternoon. The CO went to see Paddy Devlin (SDLP). The cars were blocking Kashmir Rd, Bombay St and Waterville St. This was actually more of a nuisance to the locals than to us. There was a lot of verbal abuse, whistle blowing, bin lid banging etc.

L/Cpl Emberson:

The Clonard becomes a 'no-go' area! It was never going to be tolerated by HQNI and I recall about a week later a mini-Motorman took place at about 0430 in the morning when we went back in complete with loads of Pigs and combat digger to lift out the burned cars and have the Bn in support – it all went (disappointingly!) peacefully!

An attempt was made to provoke over reaction by some minor stone throwing by kids quickly stopped by the women. There was a small amount of jostling and some photographs of patrols were taken, the usual attempt to provoke reaction along with the threats that 'we're going to have a go at you'. The boys behaved very well. The trouble is only in the Bombay St area and outside that area there is not much interest in the whole affair.

An RUC, Patrick McNulty, was killed by PIRA gunmen in Londonderry. He was in civvies taking his car to a garage, presumably well planned, as are most RUC hits.

A postman is VSI after being shot in Co. Londonderry.
Several HV fired at Monagh. No cas, 2 x 7.62 returned, NHC.

Friday 28th January

R&R!! until 1ˢᵗ Feb. 0745 fly from Aldergrove to Heathrow.
Meanwhile life goes on:
Clonard blocked off by many vehicles in protest over Moyner's death.
5lbs of Frangex, 5 lbs n/k found in a car on St Katherines St.
15 x HV fired at a B Coy patrol, no cas, 1 x 7.62 returned. They must be getting pissed off being used as for target practice.
15 x 5.56 empty cases found.
A sniper scope and ammo found in the Ardoyne.
Small explosion in the Polytechnic, no cas.

Saturday 29th January

1 x LV fired at B Coy foot patrol in Willow St. Two gunmen seen to run to Divis Flats. 4 x 7.62 returned, no cas, NHC.
1 x HV fired at Sp Coy in Springmartin Rd, 4 x 7.62 returned no cas.
2 x 10lb devices neutralised by Felix in the city centre. One hijacked car partially detonated (det only) and burnt out the vehicle in Great Victoria St.

Sunday 30th January. Bloody Sunday fifth anniversary.

A man was kneecapped in the Shankhill, NSI.
A 10 to 15 lb bomb destroyed a paint shop on the Crumlin Rd. Three civvy cas, NSI.
A small device exploded in a derelict on the Crumlin Rd, no cas.
A device consisting of 5-7 lbs of Co-op plus 85 3inch nails was neutralised in a pub on Lady's Rd. The fuze had failed.

A man lost his leg in a booby trap device at his house in Fairyknowe Gardens, VSI.

A march of about two thousand went off peacefully in Londonderry.

Monday 31st January

1 x HV fired at Sp Coy base, no cas.

A male body, James Moorehead of the UDA, was found on the Antrim Rd with severe head wounds. Killed by the UVF.

0530 all barricades in the Clonard were removed by us without incident.

5 lb bomb defused in Lurgan.

5 x HV fired at a foot patrol in Strabane, no cas.

Tuesday 1st February

A man was kneecapped in Twinbrook.

1 x LV fired at a sangar in the city centre.

1 x LV fired from Artillery Flats at a mobile in North Queen St. No cas.

Returned from R&R, landed at Aldergrove 1930. Glum. Snow.

Wednesday 2nd February

On patrol 1730-2000.

1 x LV fired a C/S 3 sangar. We were on foot in Springfield Drive/ Forfar St as it happened, heard a shot in that area not far from me. No strike found, no cas.

A man was stabbed in Springfield Rd, he lives in Cupar St, taken to RVH.

PIRA again threatens to step up anti SF campaign.

An American industrialist, Jeffrey Agate, was killed by PIRA in Londonderry.

CSE show in the cookhouse. Strippers. Highly entertaining as the manager tried to stop the Toms groping and me from photographing, both doomed to failure.

Lt. Nick O'Connor recalls escorting the Showgirls… Fortunately for us OC D Company was more enlightened.

They were called CSE Shows. Combined Services Entertainment Shows. They were booked as Go Go dancers.

I looked after them on their 'tour'. On the way up to Maj Harvey (Whiterock base?) bottles were thrown at the Pig. They shit themselves. I reassured them that it was all quite normal and there was nothing to worry about. They were not convinced.

On arrival at Harvey's location I took them in to be introduced. They were ill at ease. Harvey was in the Officers' Mess reading the Times.

'Who are these people?' asked the Maj.

'They are the Go Go dancers, sir,' I told him.

'Why are they here?'

'Well... to Go Go dance, sir.'

'What does that involve? Oh well never matter... get on with it.'

Harvey then stuck his head back in the Times. In the same movement, he looked over the paper again and said to me, 'I see Prophet that ....(some Paddy).... has been done for GBH.' Before I could engage in this exchange of pleasantries, one of the Go Go dancers interjected…

'I've been done for that, Gobbling Behind Hedges.'

Without so much as a 'by your leave' the Major stuck his head back in the Times, cleared his throat, and said, 'They don't belong in here, Prophet. I think the Sergeants' Mess is more appropriate.'

I deposited them at the Sergeants' Mess portacabin. Within minutes its windows were rattling, there was steam coming out of the chimney and there was an echo redolent to that of the local women banging dustbin lids.
Halcyon days.

Thursday 3rd February

March down the Falls and up Clonard protesting about PARA harassment.

MISR states that a J. Curron has been given clearance two days ago to carry out a snipe in either Dunmore St or Oranmore St. Weapon to be used possibly a .303. (MISR – Military Intelligence Source Report). Oranmore/Dunmore temporarily out of bounds.

At 1918 C/S 42L (Peter Akister) drove down Waterville St, past the school and into Bombay St and up Kashmir Rd. As it passed the school about twenty kids started shouting and jeering. The patrol drove on until about half way down Kashmir Rd. The two soldiers saw movement in the second floor window of 11 Bombay St and a person with what looked like a rifle. The vehicle stopped, the patrol cocked weapons and ran the fifty or so metres to the house. They burst in and were immediately greeted by an irate Mrs Quigley, the patrol reached the first floor but due to the torrential abuse withdrew. In Nov last this house had been sourced as a possible sniper position. On watch 1730-2130

A man was found in Glencairn St with his throat cut. Dead. Joseph Morrissey, killed by the UVF.

Friday 4th February

0530 4 x occupied house searches all NTR.
On watch 0730-1230.
10 to 15 lb car bomb was defused in the city centre.

B Coy found a .303 rifle in a derelict, it was a single shot Martini Henry. (Zulu!?)

On watch 1730-2130.

Sgt Edwards' Land Rover caught fire in Dunlewey St! It suddenly started to pour out smoke and flame from underneath.

The crew bailed out and the fire extinguished, the vehicle had to be towed back.

We are to take over command of No. 219 Springfield Rd as from Wednesday, will do twelve days there then hand over to 11 or 12 Platoon.

High power stuff – There is only one source in the Clonard and is so important that we cannot act on his info otherwise he is guaranteed to become compromised.

Heavy rain.

Minor demo by RVH, NFTR.

5 x HV fired somewhere in craphats land.

A bomb factory has been found in Liverpool, two arrested.

There has been a PIRA threat against families of Army personnel in particular PARA.

Five soldiers from the Black Watch have been sentenced to a total of eleven years in prison for planting evidence in 1975.

Saturday 5th February

On watch 0730-1230 nothing happened.

England beat Ireland 4-0.

5 x HV fired at a sangar in Sp Coy, no cas, FUNTR.

A man died of a heart attack on the Shankhill despite assistance from C/S 42A &42D.

On watch 1730-2130 nothing happened.

An RUC reservist, Robert Harrison, was shot dead by PIRA at his home.

219 Springfield Rd called us up to say that two armed men were

snooping around their alleys. L/Cpl Jeanette went to investigate and saw two men with SMGs. He called upon them to halt, they did not. He cocked his weapon and gave chase, eventually catching them. They turned out to be two policemen doing a house call. They had failed to tell us they were in the area and this very nearly cost them their lives. They were very white faced and shaken when L/Cpl Jeanette caught them. The reason he did not open fire was that he saw that they had hats on so decided to check further. That shows some restraint.

Sunday 6th February. Silver Jubilee of HM the Queen. (*Didn't get a Jubilee Medal. Damn.*)

On watch 0730-1230.

Provisional Sinn Fein torchlight procession from the Whiterock up to Clonard St, followed by the usual speeches etc. This is all about the cry for political status for prisoners.

A source has said that when one of the local top PIRA men was told of the find of the Armalites he said 'Fuck it, that's it then until they go!'

It's believed the rifles were being readied for one ambush which could have been nasty for us.

It is sourced that there is about 10 lbs of mix in the Beechmount area. Also that a new type of anti handling device cum booby trap has been invented in Long Kesh. This mainly affects Felix but we should be aware.

The procession went off NTR mainly due to the pissing down rain.

1 x HV fired at a foot patrol in the Ardoyne, no cas.

2 RUC shot in the country 1 dead, 1 VSI.

1 x HV fired at a foot patrol in Londonderry, no cas.

Several bombs defused throughout the Province.

2/Lt Warwick Stacey recalls a nasty scare:

We had a few officers from outside D Coy, including Prophet bless him, as well as the former OC of 12 Platoon, living at the mill.

Coming back early one evening to the D Coy mess I walked through the dining room to the TV room. The TV was on and blaring, and there was a body sitting lounged back on the scabby old sofa, head down, trousers unzipped and tadger out and in his right hand. He was asleep at the wheel.

Being brand new I realised the situation was quite delicate and did not want to interrupt what had already been interrupted by slumber.

I started to back out. He was roused from his nap, squinted at me, looked at his whanger, squinted at me again and said 'Who's that? The light from the room behind must have darkened my face.

I told him it was Dave Ellis, but I was not sure if he believed me.

He said, 'Don't say anything will you.'

I agreed and said, 'You can count on that. Dave Ellis's word is his bond,' and off I slunk.

I am sorry Dave. I have carried this guilt all these years.

On a positive note, you obviously were not that officer on the sofa.

We sought solace where we could find it – mostly with rigorous self-examination, Gibbo's or Jimmy Kerr's porn, and the occasional beer.

Wonderful days.

Monday 7th February

The padre said he'd been asked by a Catholic woman if it was a sin for their gunmen to kill soldiers….she was in her 50's.

RWF working on an anonymous phone call found a 0.3006 Woodmaster carbine in Turf Lodge.

6 x HV fired at Moyard (Sp Coy), no cas, FUNTR.

A man was found shot in the neck in Glencairn, he'd also had a battered head. The local press have accused 'The mad butcher of the Shankhill' for all the recent murders, Lenny Murphy and his UVF team.

1 x LV fired at a mobile in Denmark St, no cas. FUNTR. No reason why they should fire at us!

On patrol 0500-0800. Very quiet. Found a dazed motorcyclist on the Falls by the baths. Some workmen had left a hole in the road surrounded by oil lamps. However during the night they were stolen. He hit the hole, became airborne and hit a bus. Apart from bruising he was OK.

2 x petrol bombs were thrown at a mobile in North Queen St.

4 x HV fired at a pig on Antrim Rd. No cas.

Tuesday 8th February

Cpl Barber, whilst on foot patrol in a back alley behind Violet St decided to walk along one of the walls separating the alley from the back 'garden', the reason being to look into all the gardens and back rooms. However he received a rather unpleasant surprise. As he was walking along he saw an oldish Hog sitting on the privy in the back yard. No inside bogs here. The door was wide open and the light was on and he was given a full frontal as she stood up to scratch herself, go about her business and leave. All in all he thought that this was one of the nastier of his experiences in NI. C/S 41A & D tasked to escort Mr Mason the NI Secretary up the Falls Rd.

Back alley searches all NTR.

A 2lb bomb suspended in the fume filled compartment of a petrol tanker was defused by ATO. The other compartment contained about 2000 gallons of petrol. The tanker had been hijacked on the Springfield Rd and abandoned as a proxy bomb outside Musgrave St RUC station. Had it gone off it would have flattened the station and caused substantial local damage.

Two fifteen year old youths were found tied to railings on Clonard St covered in paint. Admitted to RVH for a cleanup. Just a minor punishment for petty crime.

Planned lift of the lovely Sue Devine cancelled as she'd had an argument with her mother and left home. Seen and lifted later in the day.

Men arrested for the murder of Mr Agate have put in a claim that they had been ill treated. This received more publicity than the fact that they had committed the murder. Typical.

Saw the SIB ref the man who punched L/Cpl Bell on 13 Jan. He alleges that L/Cpl Bell beat him up. The investigation of his complaint has been far more thorough than that of L/Cpl Bell's attack. We have been told to expect a series of letter bombs.

Information that the Prods are planning something has come from several sources. There are reports that Prods are mass producing homemade 9mm SMGs.

It's also been reported that 'they are just about fed up with the whole affair' and are going to have an intensive offensive against PIRA in the not too distant future. They are supposedly forming a corps of ex servicemen whose sole purpose in life is to execute known Provisionals. A fair one!

On patrol 2100-0100.

Explosion in Argyle St. A derelict house mysteriously blew up, possibly gas but unlikely as people were seen leaving there.

RUC poked around in the ruins destroying evidence and removed a gas cylinder much to the amusement of Sgt Evans and L/Cpl Doolan who were waiting for another explosion to signal the end of the DIY Felix. No one seemed very interested as there were no cas and no apparent intended target. The rest of the area was its usual quiet self.

Wednesday 9th February

On watch 0730-1130.

Took over command of 219 Springfield Road and spent a long time trying to get a workable stag cum patrol cum search routine going. Trying to man a base that should have 30 with 23 bods presents certain problems especially as commitments are increasing.

Sgt Maj Duncan's patrol found a PIRA MkX grenade on waste ground between the link fencing and the corrugated iron where

Kashmir Rd goes through the peace line. It is not known how long it has been there. Felix destroyed it in situ with a controlled explosion.

2 x LV fired at RWF in Turf Lodge, no cas FUNTR.

6 x n/k fired at D&D in New Lodge, no cas FUNTR.

On patrol 2030-2300. Pissing with rain. Did more pub visits. Still a strong smell of bleach in Bombay St. Bleach has been used in homemade explosives.

219 Springfield Rd is an old house fortified with rocket screens and two sangars. It is on the corner of Springfield Rd/Cupar St. There is rather spartan accommodation for about 30 troops. It's equipped with an Int cum briefing room, ops room, kitchen, cookhouse, showers etc and 6 x 4 man rooms plus a number of smaller rooms one of which is mine and one Sgt MacNaughton's. To work from here for four months would be ideal.

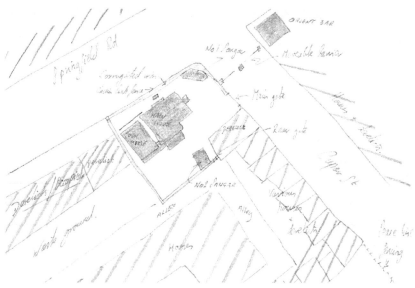

219 Springfield Rd plan.

219 Springfield Rd.

Thursday 10th February

Sat on the ops desk till 0400. Eventually managed to get a system going that left the search team free of guard duties and yet did not knacker the rest. We are waiting for the CO to arrive and tell us to change it all. Still pissing with rain.

Balcombe St bombers have been sentenced to life imprisonment with a recommendation to serve a minimum of 30 years.

There has been no local reaction but no doubt it will get a hysterical reception in the local comics.

Author's note:

In 1974 and 1975, London was subjected to a 14-month campaign of gun and bomb attacks by the Provisional IRA. Some 40 bombs exploded in London, killing 35 people and injuring many more. In one incident the Guinness Book of Records cofounder and Conservative political activist Ross McWhirter was assassinated; he had offered a £50,000 reward to anyone willing to inform the security forces of IRA activity.

After serving 23 years in English prisons, the four men were transferred to the high security wing of Portlaoise Prison, 50 miles (80 km) west of Dublin, in early 1998. They were presented by Gerry Adams to the 1998 Sinn Féin Ard Fheis as 'our Nelson Mandelas', and were released together with Brendan Dowd and Liam Quinn in 1999 as part of the Good Friday Agreement.

On patrol 1630-1730. Quiet due to rain. Found seven heavy coach bolts of the type used in Claymores in the Beechmount.

A mobile found a .45 Magnum empty case in Iris St.

The routine we are running is:

Patrol 1	Patrol 2	Guard
Search team + 2	Pln Cmd / Sgt +7	6

Ops briefing etc.

Int cell + Pte Allen (broken arm.)

Patrol 1 does all searches and alternates patrols with Patrol 2.

Patrol 2 and Guard exchange 6 pax every 24 hours.

2 pax from Patrol 1 (i.e. those not search trained) are rotated.

Guard does two and a half hours on and five off for twenty four hours.

Changeover every twenty four hours.

The disadvantage of this is that NCOs do stag duties in the sangars and Patrol 2 has 2 NCOs as well as Lt./Sgt.

This works OK with twenty three bods, any less and we'll struggle.

D&D had a good arms find.

A patrol of RWF had to fire 15 x BR to extricate themselves from a cul-de-sac whilst being heavily stoned. It all started from an attempt to recover a stolen car. No serious cas.

Evening patrols NTR.

Looking up Springfield Rd from 219 sangar. Note pub bomb watch with two crutches. And the rain!

Friday 11th February

Anniversary of the death of hunger striker Frank Stagg. In April 1973, Stagg was arrested for planning bombing attacks in the UK. He was tried and given a ten-year sentence. On 14 December 1975, Stagg embarked on a second hunger strike (the first having been unsuccessful in meeting his demands for repatriation) in HMP Wakefield and died on 12 February 1976 after 62 days on hunger strike.

Occupied house search by C/S 41A & D NTR.

Two prominent businessmen were shot at in their houses on the Malone Rd area. One missed, the other was hit in the neck and is NSI.

Three armed men attempted to rob a garage on the Lisburn Rd but came unstuck when the proprietor aged in his 60's produced a shotgun and blasted them. Two fled leaving behind one dead.

1920 heard an explosion in the city centre, turned out to be a car bomb in Great Patrick St. One man injured in the hand. Could have been an own goal or trap, details to follow hopefully.

1 x LV heard in Whiterock. NTR.

41A recovered a burnt out car that had been stolen.

The car bomb was confirmed as a booby trap, two men taken to hospital, both NSI. The bomb was quite small, 2-3lbs.

An eight year old boy was slightly wounded when two gunmen forced their way into his home and grabbed his mother. They fired a number of rounds and fled.

L/Cpl Sullivan had a stroke of bad luck. He is due to go on R&R this morning and he got a phone call saying that his fiancée has just had her appendix removed.

Incredible but true

The CO's rover group were moving in a pig up the Springfield Rd when the CO noticed that they were not wearing helmets. It is usual to wear them in a pig in case of crash or bomb. He pondered on this for a while and announced that the entire crew (less the poor driver) would put their hands on their heads in order to protect the top of their heads in case they got blown up. He must be under the illusion that that would really work if the pig was mined!

He came to 219 and announced that we should not wear waterproof jackets when on foot patrol when it is raining. However we can wear them under our smocks. Reasons being that they are noisy and shiny and impractical. But they do keep the radios dry. He has obviously not been out for two or three hours, back in for a couple and back out again and so on for days with no drying facilities. (*No Gore-Tex in those days.*)

One of the Toms muttered, "Do we need to put our socks on over our boots then?" Heard on the net: "The time has come, the bells do chime, for us to go to two one nine!"

On patrol 2200-0000. Drizzle, virtually deserted.

I discovered a girl guides den off Springfield Avenue when a tiny kid ran into me after breaking a window. I got him to take me to where he did the deed and found a load of guides in full kit puffing away. Anniversary of the death of hunger striker Frank Stagg. It looks like he died in vain as there was not much news coverage.

Saturday 12th February

A Sgt in the Coldstream Guards died in a road accident in Londonderry.

A number of RPG launchers and rockets were found in the Republic.

An RUC man was killed in Co. Antrim by shots fired from a passing van.

A source has said that women in long coats were carrying weapons in the Springfield and Falls Roads. Wow! Expect an attempt to set up a patrol. As usual nothing came of it.

Sp Coy found a pistol and 20 x .22 in a planned search.

The Fleas

41A&D carried out a planned search in a house yesterday. It was particularly nasty, even by Belfast standards, and this morning there were two cases of flea bites in 219. By the evening half the platoon had flea bites. It took several irate phone calls from me to Tac before the QM sent up a crate of DDT. Needless to say the Toms went berserk with it, people were beginning to resemble snowmen and the entire living quarters was covered with DDT. Hopefully that will fix the problem otherwise the building will have to be fumigated which means evacuating it for two days or so. *To be continued…*

The Pye net talkthrough went u/s at 2300 so my patrol was cancelled. No great loss as yet again it's pissing down with rain and of course we can't take our waterproof out!

A source has said that PIRA have probably replaced the weapons and explosives losses that they have incurred recently.

The tanker bomb that Felix defused earlier in the week was a very poorly made device, it was constructed along very similar lines to the one found on the Whiterock Rd on 14 Dec. and the one found in Ballymurphy on 13 Jan. The bomb consisted of about 2lbs of Co-op suspended inside the tanker. The detonator had gone off but failed to fire the main charge.

Clonard accused us of whitewashing a black taxi…??

Two men in their 30's admitted themselves to the RVH after having blue (2 PARA colour!) paint poured over them.

Sunday 13th February

We have been informed that all petrol tankers should only have one person in the cab.

Gerry Adams is due for release tomorrow, an ex Belfast Brigade commander so we were told.

It is believed that the IRSP are leaning heavily on the PIRA in the Whiterock, it is known that some PIRA men are in fear of their lives and are using women to carry weapons. The theory being that the woman walks about 30m behind the man and if any trouble crops up she can give him the weapon. So?

1 x LV fired at the RUC Andersonstown, no cas, FUNTR.

One of the priests in the Monastery put in a complaint against Cpl Blowers, saying that he had held a civvy up against the railings on the Falls. NFTR. On patrol 2130-2359

A businessman was attacked by a bomb and pistol on the Antrim Rd. No cas but his house was damaged.

Source says it's unlikely anyone will have a go at us until the last week or so of the tour.

BRs fired at a crowd in T. Lodge to disperse stone throwers.

Fleas contd

The Doc and a bird from the local health authority came to find our fleas. The Doc laughed himself silly when he saw the DDT all over the place. He reckoned we'd used enough to decontaminate the battalion. On the bright side no one comes to visit us.

Pte Anderton captured a flea from his neck on a piece of masking tape.

A car bomb was defused in Hollywood.

Monday 14th February

Despite the DDT more fleas continue to attack – is fumigation our only hope? The captured flea, still alive and struggling, was taken under escort by Saracen to some mysterious department for analysis.

0425 4 x LV fired at McRory Park (A Coy), the firing point was believed to be the cemetery. A patrol was sent out to investigate, saw a suspicious person by a gravestone and opened fire with 2 x 7.62. No hits claimed, no cas.

RRF fired 3 x BR to extricate themselves from a crowd in Turf Lodge.

A suspect stolen car was found by B Coy by Dunville Park, it was treated as a come on and Felix was tasked. He was not happy with it so set off a controlled explosion which burnt out the car. Unlucky for someone.

A man was arrested for failing to give details and attempted assault on L/Cpl Gibbins. He was taken to Tac HQ.

There were a number of cases of women refusing to open their coats for scrutiny. This is OK during the day when we can get a WRAC to do it. For some reason they, WRAC, don't come out to play at night with the result that I arrested three grots on the Falls Rd and took them to Tac where they spent the regulation four hours, all rather pointless for them.

Int forecast…No real idea of what is being planned in the Province. It is thought that an attack may be made against plain clothed military personnel working from 0. We have been asked to look out for dicking or suspect come-ons especially involving kids to produce a set up.

We've received a fair amount of abuse, whistling etc. from various hogs in the Cavendish as a result of our purge against females with coats.

In Dublin Seamus Twomey, Chief of Staff PAC PIRA, has said that PIRA intend turning London into a battlefield.

Tuesday 15th February

A suspect device was dealt with by Felix in A Coy's area.

1 x LV fired at a foot patrol in the Lower Falls. The round tore the waterproof (why was he wearing one?!) and flak jacket of the Tom. Seen below wearing his waterproof over his smock.

FUIHP into several houses all NTR, several suspects were lifted. B Coy leaping around for a bit. Initial reports were that the shot came from Raglan St. See the strike mark above.

We arrested two more females for failing to open their coats, this resulted in a certain amount of verbal hostility. It's my belief that they have been instructed to do this deliberately to mess us about, when in fact the reverse is the case. I expect they'll get bored with it in the end. Tac was very worried throughout the day that someone was going to ambush a patrol or RUC leaving their location. As a result we have had to spend a fair amount of time hanging around 'hijack corner'. Caught a few yoblets throwing bricks.

On patrol 2130-2359

0630 search of business premises in Forfar St NTR.

Rain all day.

A 10lb booby trapped bomb was defused by the Crumlin Rd.

Wednesday 16th February

0230-0530 put in a house search in Sp Coy's area to help them out.

A courting couple in Londonderry were shot up as they were having it off in a car. The man was taken to hospital to have glass removed from his body…arse? NSI.

As a result of a robot telephone call a search was mounted in 47 Lucknow St. A .3006 Savage (Winchester action) with a telescopic sight was found. Also found in the house were some documents and tapes. As these were being removed Mr Kelly went mad so perhaps they will be of some use. A bag smelling very heavily of marzipan was also found. As the search team went in with the RUC rent-a-mob appeared in quick time with the usual whistle blowing and bin lid banging.

Follow up searches went into the Quinn's house in Dunmore St and the SP betting shop in Kashmir Rd, NTR. They were all accompanied by rent-a-crowd who were not pleased.

The initial telephone call said that two men, one armed had gone into this house. At least someone in the Clonard doesn't like PIRA!

L/Cpl Emberson recalls:

There also seems to be another story missing (but it may not have been 10 Plt) unless I've got my memories confused. As well as the 'Armalites under the sofa' incident on the 24th of January where (allegedly) the bonus outcome was a tired search dog getting a good kip I recall a separate event (but again it may be a memory failure).

One quiet afternoon we were sat in the Int with PC MacFarlane perfecting his tea drinking skills. PC MacFarlane was a big fat plod who epitomised why the RUC had had to call the Army in but was generally well liked as he would do some shopping for the Toms, was not averse to smuggling in a few extra beers for the lads and occasionally offered some magazines that the Gibbins-Kerr cartel could not provide.

I'm sure that his frequent visits to the Int were only 50% about the tea we provided and the other 50% about studying our Photographic PIRA Orbats for onward transmission to UDA friends but I may be being cynical. Anyway at some stage a message came over his RUC net saying all C/S should avoid the Clonard as information to the confidential telephone from a member of the public passing by had said two rifles had been moved into an address given in clear over the radio.

I recall it as either Lucknow or Cupar St with 47 Lucknow sticking in my head – anyway it was the familial home of the Kelly's (as in Gerard the Old Bailey bomber and frequent escapee from various prisons). I later found out that the information was given by an SB or Army source to his/her handler but needed a cover story before it was acted on so the source – a member of PIRA – was not fingered. Sending it over the net in clear (which was known to be monitored by PIRA) was thought to be a good red herring. Anyway after discussion (was it a come on? if it wasn't it was now you've sent it out in clear etc.) PC MacFarlane insisted he was going round to search the house and demanded an Army escort.

Eventually a patrol was dispatched which I accompanied and 2 (?) Armalites were found badly hidden in a roll of lino in the back room. Present in the house was a woman who was Gerard Kelly's wife – I recall her as Isobel/Isabella Kelly but Gerard's current wife (he's now an MLA! - Member of the Legislative Assembly) is listed as Margaret. Gerard was OTR at the time I believe. We duly arrested her and I remember photographing her wearing a sullen scowl and those (joke) paper bags we used to put over hands for later forensic tests. I believe at her trial the defence was 'I went out to the shops and seconds after I got back the Brits turned up, I'd left the yard door and the back door open when I went out so someone else must have left the guns there' and the forensic evidence from the bags being (as always) useless she was duly acquitted.

On patrol 1530-1800 and 2230-0040.

Heard an explosion to the south at 2315, later confirmed as being in a scrap yard in the Village area. It didn't sound very big.

Ref B Coy's contact, the Tom was facing the firing point and turned just as the round was fired. It zipped across his back cutting his FJ. Had he not turned it would have hit him in the centre of his chest.

He was either knocked over by the round or fainted… according to his mates!

Cpl Robinson found a pair of binos and some electrical equipment including a radio control receiver in Kelly's Bar in Sp Coy's area. (Ably assisted so I am told by the OC, CSM etc. of SP Coy.)

Thursday 17th February

The round fired at B Coy has been identified as a .30.

The rifle found yesterday was a .308 with a conversion kit to 7.62, a very accurate weapon – better than an Armalite.

A few known PIRA men were seen together in the West Belfast Social Club just before the message came in about the rifle. Possibly discussing the movement of the weapon.

Mrs Kelly is being spoken to at Castlreagh by the CID, they are particularly interested in the explosives traces found.

An IED was found by the RRF in the Falls Rd which resulted in the road being blocked for some time.

D&D had a 'gun battle' in the New Lodge Rd, no cas.

Two bombs exploded in the Falls Rd bus depot doing a small amount of damage, the area had been cleared.

On patrol 2230-0040, heavy rain, very quiet.

There is a plan to lift Hugh O'Neill when he's on the move with others and his hands must be bagged. This had come from Brigade

Int. All rather vague but someone has been doing their homework we are told.

As expected the CO came round, now that we are declared flea free, and stuck his nose into our routines. We know he has pressure from above but he is becoming a bit unpopular by constantly criticising and bollocking people without asking for reasons why things are being done.

The CO did not endear himself to L/Cpl 'Baggy' Baggart who was left behind for about half an hour on his own in the Ballymurphy at night when the CO's R Group drove off, a completely inexcusable thing to happen. Apparently L/Cpl B spent the half hour shouting to imaginary patrol members in an attempt to make it seem that he was in company. He was eventually reunited with the R Group and I believe that he made his feelings known. I am told that he used a red telephone box to call in to Tac HQ.

If only we'd get a word of encouragement from time to time instead of grunts and bollockings he'd have a happier Battalion and that's not just my opinion.

Roll on Depot PARA!

Friday 18th February

Morning search NTR.

A number of buses were hijacked and set on fire in the Turf Lodge.

A proxy bomb was planted in the Markets.

An anon bomb warning was given that there was a bomb in Smithfield in the city centre, not far from the telex, and was defused by Felix.

During the afternoon a patrol from Sp Coy stopped a taxi and whilst P checking the occupants the patrol commander was assaulted. Rent a crowd appeared on the scene fairly rapidly and kept up some abuse. When the crowd melted away fifteen shots were fired from three different firing points. It then appears that a ten man patrol skirmished into the Turf Lodge in hot pursuit firing 55 x 7.62 as they did so. The press claim that over 200 rounds were fired. Lots of stoning and bottling took place too.

A blast bomb was thrown at a patrol in Springfield Parade, no cas.

6 x HV fired in Turf Lodge, no cas.

An empty beer barrel was destroyed by Felix in Conway St after a patrol declared it suspicious.

A meat van was hijacked in the Falls/Leeson St area. The driver was removed and blindfolded and the vehicle driven away. He was told where he could collect it a few hours later. The usual routine.

It's thought that there will be a wave of hijackings as a preliminary to a new bombing campaign in the city centre.

In Sp Coys shooting there were no cas and NHC. Not very good results having fired 55 rounds!

More on the shooting. The man who assaulted the commander was taken away in a Saracen. It was then that two different patrols came under fire from three different locations. It appears that a total of 20 x HV were fired from these locations at both patrols. Whilst assaulting the firing points the patrol fired 55 rounds as suppressing fire to keep the gunmen's heads down. In this they succeeded.

Saturday 19th February. My birthday, number 26.

3 x HV fired at the D&Ds. No cas.

2 x HV fired at Sp Coy patrol just north of the Bullring, 2 x 7.62 returned, no cas.

A man was arrested in Beechmount by C/S 42 on suspicion after a helicopter spotted a red VW moving away from that area.

It appears that in yesterday's shooting three rounds were fired from one position, six from another and eleven at a patrol during the follow up.

The round fired the other day at B Coy was from an M1 carbine and believed fired by the IRSP, an unusual occurrence.

The D&Ds had an intruder on their radio net, suspected as IRA asking for details of a Stop 1 vehicle.

It's known that there is about seven hundred pounds of explosives in Belfast ready for immediate use.

Sources say there are two rifles at large in the Beechmount/Cavendish area. Four sources have said that PIRA are out to get civilianised military at Springfield Rd police station.

On patrol 1400-1630. All quiet.

Could see the smoke from burning buses on the Donegal Rd, now almost a daily event. The Falls Rd bus depot was badly damaged by fire, six buses destroyed in the evening.

Pte Ware was refused service in a shop when he went in to buy fags. The shopkeeper said sorry that she wasn't allowed to serve SF. We left and a few minute later a woman stopped us and gave him a packet that she said she thought he had dropped. She was in the shop when we were refused so she must have taken pity on us and bought them herself. No one had dropped any so it was a really nice gesture.

We received a slight stoning in Beechmount Pass. A large spotty yob went very white when he was caught and told he'd have his skull split if he even looked at us again. We didn't catch anyone red handed but I think we got the message over.

It's been announced that the RUC are to have much more control over the Army's routine in the City. They are now supposed to vet all our search, patrol routines etc. They can be seen belting through the hard areas in armoured Land Rovers, but only it seems when the army is about. I wish we had their overtime rates of pay!

A man was beaten up on the Falls, his face was rather a mess. He was P checked, found to be PIRA so no one was bothered.

A man, Brian Canavan was shot dead by the UDA in north Belfast.

It's believe that D2 PIRA are behind the recent assassination attempts on industrialists.

An unsatisfactory birthday.

We shall all be very glad to leave this place.

It's thought that Sp Coy may have hit someone in their recent contact as a PIRA oriented nurse has been spotted doing her rounds which is unusual. Why not follow her?

The author on his birthday. Pte Gordon Fawcett taking the piss.

Sunday 20th February

Leave 219 Springfield Rd for NHSt. We will now spend the rest of the tour alternating between patrols and guard.

As a footnote to our time there, it is rumoured that the IRA attempted to dig a tunnel under 219 with the intention of planting a bomb and sending it skywards. Maybe they did and it hasn't exploded, rather akin to the 'Birdcage 3' mine on Messines ridge, laid by the British in 1916 and which lay in waiting until 17th June 1955 when lightning hit a pylon built over the site causing the mine to explode. Much to the surprise of the landowner.

Sp Coy dealt with an IED.

Had a very welcome sauna, shower and dhobi when we got back. None of the Toms seem sad to be leaving 219. Cancel my earlier remark about being happy to stay there for the tour!

The RWF had 1 x .3006 fired at a patrol leaving Ft Monagh, 1 x 7.62 returned, no cas.

Yesterday a total of twelve buses were burnt out in two separate incidents. Also Sp Coy had 4 x HV fired at them from two firing points, 11 x 7.62 returned, NHC, no cas.

5 x LV fired by Kelly's Bar, later a man was admitted to the RVH with GSW to both legs.

An RUC constable narrowly escaped when a booby trap exploded.

As a result of the follow up to a shooting a clip of .3006 Garrand rounds were found, the constable picked them up and bang.

It's thought that PIRA are looking for a settlement and may attempt to negotiate from a 'position of strength' by starting more bombings.

In Londonderry troops found about 80 lbs of explosives.

A man was kneecapped in Sandy Row.

4 x HV fired at the D&D in the Ardoyne, no cas, 4 x 7.62 returned. In the follow up 3 x 5.56 and 1 x .3006 empty cases were found in Etna Drive. A 1lb bomb with electric initiation was found by the firing point. It's common to lure troops to a bomb following a shooting. Sp Coy beware.

In 1977 so far nineteen people have been murdered in Northern Ireland compared with eighteen in Glasgow over the same period. Not so much shooting, bombing and rioting though.

On watch 1730-2130.

A woman was arrested by C/S 42L for failing to open her coat for inspection. Nice one Peter!

As a party from the Labour Party National Executive are visiting the Ballymurphy no troop movement is allowed whilst they are there. Really magic.

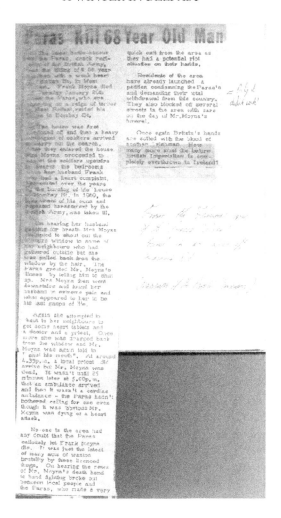

Monday 21st February

A man was kneecapped in Turf Lodge, he was set upon by ten men, made to lay face down in an alley and was shot once in the back of the knee. NSI.

An M1 rifle and a .303 rifle were found in N. Belfast.

A device consisting of a MkX mortar, det, fuze, command wire and petrol was neutralised in the Ballymurphy.

A bus conductor had his takings stolen when his bus was hijacked on the Springfield Rd. He and the bus were later released. There was an explosion in Windsor E. Belfast. 1-2 oz of explosives went off under the wheel arch of a car. Seemingly a misfire.

Search in Cavendish St NTR.

On watch 0730-1230, nothing happened.

The PIRA today claimed responsibility for the "shooting of a soldier of The Parachute Regiment on Tuesday". (Irish News 22/2/77). Shooting 'at' would have been more accurate. This is in contradiction to the firm belief by Int that it was an OIRA/ IRSP job. It could mean that D2 PIRA are becoming more active, they may attempt more cross boundary shootings in the future, i.e. over the Falls. It's assumed that they know where unit and sub unit boundaries are and would be aware of the restrictions of follow ups over these boundaries. Most of 2LI's contacts have been thus.

An SB source says PIRA intend to intensify their campaign and that they believe they can win. We often wonder whether anyone really believes much of the drivel coming from these sources!

2 Queens took over from 1RWF in the Lodge and Andersonstown.

Another man was kneecapped in Dunmurray. His was the 23rd kneecapping this year. Ouch.

A soldier had a narrow escape when a booby trap went off in Londonderry.

There was also a robbery in a UDR man's house, his SLR, a .22 rifle, ammunition and uniform were stolen. This was in Co. Londonderry.

So far this year thirty three buses have been burnt and destroyed.

RESTRICTED

17. If you have to challenge a person who is acting suspiciously you must do so in a firm, distinct, voice saying "HALT - HANDS UP."

   a. If he halts you are to say "STAND STILL AND KEEP YOUR HANDS UP."

   b. Ask him why he is there, and if not satisfied call your Commander immediately and hand the person over to him.

18. If the person does not halt at once, you are to challenge again saying "HALT - HANDS UP" and, if the person does not halt on your second challenge, you are to cock your weapon, apply the safety catch and shout: "STAND STILL I AM READY TO FIRE."

19. The rules covering the circumstances for opening fire are described in paragraphs 8 - 14. If the circumstances do not justify opening fire, you will do all you can to stop and detain the person without opening fire.

20. At a road block/check, you will NOT fire on a vehicle simply because it refused to stop. If a vehicle does not halt at a road block/check, note its description make, registration number and direction of travel.

21. In all circumstances where you have challenged and the response is not satisfactory, you will summon your Commander at the first opportunity.

Revised November 1972

RESTRICTED

RESTRICTED

Army Code No. 70771

Instructions by the Director of Operations for Opening Fire in Northern Ireland

1. These instructions are for the guidance of Commanders and troops operating collectively or individually. When troops are operating collectively soldiers will only open fire when ordered to do so by the Commander on the spot.

General Rules

2. Never use more force than the minimum necessary to enable you to carry out your duties.

3. Always first try to handle the situation by other means than opening fire if you have to fire
   a. Fire only aimed shots.
   b. Do not fire more rounds than are absolutely necessary to achieve your aim.

4. Your magazine/bolt must always be loaded with live ammunition and be fitted to the weapon. Unless you are about to open fire no live round is to be carried in the breech, and the working parts must be forward. Company Commanders and above may, when circumstances in their opinion warrant such action, order weapons to be cocked, with a round in the breech where appropriate, and the safety catch at safe.

5. Automatic fire may be used against identified targets in the same circumstances as single shots if in the opinion of the Commander on the spot, it is the

RESTRICTED

RESTRICTED

minimum force required and no other weapon can be employed as effectively. Because automatic fire scatters it is not to be used where persons not using firearms are in, or may be close to, the line of fire.

Warning before firing

6. Whenever possible a warning should be given before you open fire. The only circumstances in which you may open fire without giving warning are described in paras. 13, 14 and 15 below.

7. A warning should be as loud as possible, preferably by loud hailer. It must:
   a. Give clear orders to stop attacking or to halt, as appropriate.
   b. State that fire will be opened if the orders are not obeyed.

You may fire after due warning

8. Against a person carrying what you can positively identify as a firearm,* but only if you have reason to think that he is about to use it for offensive purposes
   and
he refuses to halt when called upon to do so and there is no other way of stopping him.

9. Against a person throwing a petrol bomb if petrol bomb attacks continue in your area against troops and civilians or against property, if his action is likely to endanger life.

10. Against a person attacking or destroying property or stealing firearms or explosives, if his action is likely to endanger life.

   *NOTE: "Firearm" includes a grenade, nail bomb or gelignite type bomb

RESTRICTED

RESTRICTED

11. Against a person who, though he is not at present attacking has:
   a. in your sight killed or seriously injured a member of the security forces or a person whom it is your duty to protect
   and
   b. not halted when called upon to do so and cannot be arrested by any other means.

12. If there is no other way to protect yourself or those whom it is your duty to protect from the danger of being killed or seriously injured.

You may fire without warning

13. When hostile firing is taking place in your area, and a warning is impracticable.
   a. against a person using a firearm* against you or those whom it is your duty to protect
   or
   b. against a person carrying what you can positively identify as a firearm* if he is clearly about to use it for offensive purposes.

14. At a vehicle if the occupants open fire or throw a bomb at you or those whom it is your duty to protect, or are clearly about to do so.

15. If there is no other way to protect yourself or those whom it is your duty to protect from the danger of being killed or seriously injured.

Action by guards and at road blocks/checks

16. Where warnings are called for they should be in the form of specific challenges as set out in paragraphs 17 and 18.

RESTRICTED

The Yellow Card.

Army Code No. 70771, Ministry of Defence © Crown Copyright 1972.

Tuesday 22nd February

Ptes Mortonson and Ware demobbed after three years' service. Thanks lads, a job well done, Good luck.

Warwick Stacey's comment:
I remember a Tom telling me he was leaving the Army around this time (may have been one of those two). I suggested he might like to reconsider as he would miss the rich and colourful tapestry of life in the PARAs.
His reply was superb.
Whenever I think I that I want to return to the Regiment I will go out in the garden after dark and dig a trench all night while the wife runs the hose over me. If I still miss the Army after that I might re-enlist'. He did leave the Army.
I saw him in 1980 in 2 PARA's Ops room in Ballykinler. We both agreed that Airborne masochism always wins.

On watch 0730-1230.
C/S 43E recovered a car wanted as a result of a Rat Trap called by city centre RUC.
A stolen car used in an armed robbery of a post office in Andersonstown was recovered with the driver by Sp Coy.
Two incendiary bombs were found and neutralised in a supermarket in Castle St. Only minor damage was caused by the one that went off.
A clip of Garrand .3006 ammo was found, booby trapped, in Londonderry. Underneath the clip was a microswitch that was connected to a nearby 5lb charge. It was safely neutralised.
B Coy found 1 x .22 pistol, 100 x .22 rounds, 90 x 9mm rounds. Eight people were arrested in connection with this find.
All the spate of kneecappings over the past few days have been dealt out by PIRA. The victims all punished, so they say for stealing cars. Maybe they won't admit that some are for disloyalty, according to Int.
A patrol was tasked to lift someone this pm on request from RUC, however he had flown as he was expecting a kneecapping for stealing

a car. Why not just get a taxi or bus?? Or walk?

A suspect car bomb was dealt with on the Monagh roundabout.

On watch 1730-2130. Nothing happened in the battalion area.

On watch 0130-0730 Wed, not really worth going to bed! Don MacNaughton is on R&R so I'm a bit pushed for duties.

Only three weeks to go.

A proxy car bomb exploded in Antrim causing minimal damage and no cas. A very quiet day, the first for a long time with no shootings in the Province.

Wednesday 23rd February

On watch 0130-0730.

Start mobiles at 1300. Ref the shooting of Cpl Porter on the 18th December, it appears that this could have been a negligent discharge (ND). Due to warnings of a sniping threat the A Coy patrols were moving with their weapons 'made ready'. It seems that a member of the patrol had an ND and then continued firing to cover up his mistake. This cannot be proved but seems a possibility as no organisation has claimed responsibility which they always do.

A search in Cavendish St was NTR. This was carried out at the request of the SB and had hopes as the occupier is IO of D2 PIRA.

5 x HV fired at a patrol in the Creggan area of Londonderry. No cas.

1 x HV fired at a patrol in Turf Lodge, no cas.

A source report says that a bombing run due to be made in early February was cancelled due to patrol activity. It also states that the only people who are really active in D2 PIRA are Kelly, Mehan, Carsons and Gerard Moyna (PIRA and later RIRA) plus two NK females. It's also been reported that William Kelly has a new pistol.

Apparently G. Moyna tried to kill an RUC by shooting him with a pistol in the back of the head, the gun misfired and Moyna ran away. The policeman reported that he knew nothing about it. In 1973 he earned the nickname 'Posty' by attempting to post a bomb through the slits of a pig. Quite brave actually.

A businessman, JP Hill, was killed by a shotgun attack in his home in Londonderry. He was a company director and a Major in the UDR.

Another businessman was shot and wounded on the Antrim Rd. NSI.

There was a bomb scare in a hotel on the Antrim Rd. Declared false after a couple of controlled explosions.

Thursday 24th February

On patrol 0100-0500 Nothing at all happened. Very cold.

2 RUC were shot in Lurgan, one, Harold Cobb, died immediately the other is VSI. About twenty rounds were fired by gunmen, they fired into their backs from about twenty five feet. Brave lads.

The Queens Regiment found a Lewis gun in the Turf Lodge, it was in poor condition but in working order. There was also 35 x .303 and a drum magazine with it.

The outlook for the next few days/weeks is anyone's guess. There have been no major indications of any planned activity by any of the players. It just remains for us to stay alert for the next three weeks. We must continue to remind ourselves that the PIRA are the ones who initiate 99% of incidents. They can chose the time, the place, the type of incident and have their escape routes all worked out. It is up to us and our skill to prevent a snipe being made by alertness, smartness and going through the correct drills at all times. Now is the time to kick a few arses, especially as we are now only doing mobile patrols. There has been a tendency for the crews of mobile patrols to switch off. We have had one or two cases in the Company of heads nodding… not in 10 platoon yet I am happy to say.

A large car bomb was defused in Antrim, no further details.

Pte Adams (HQ Coy) had an ND with an SMG in the unloading bay at Tac HQ.

Nick O'Connor comments:

Pte Adams had the ND (Negligent Discharge) in the front Sanger at Battalion HQ.

Major Pat Wood, the rather disliked Battalion Second in Command, Captain John Reith, the Adjutant (my mate then) and myself were in the Adjutant's Office in the Springfield Road. There was what I discerned as a low velocity shot from the area of the front sangar (just outside the window).

Pat Wood thought we had been shot at. I said unlikely and more probably an ND in the front sangar. Pat Wood turned on me, as oft times was the case, and yelled, 'If ever we want military advice, Prophet, you're the last fucking person we'll ever ask.' Thicko Pat didn't like officers with degrees.

Five minutes later they were filling in the ND report. The first thing Pat Wood asked John Reith was, 'When was the last time Adams fired his weapon?' (We were supposed to fire on the ranges regularly to keep in practice.)

'Fucking obvious,' I said, 'about 5 minutes ago.' Pat Wood went berserk.

John Reith quite politely said, 'Just get the fuck out of here.'

Such was the state of apoplexy into which Pat Wood had descended, that as I left the Adjutant's Office, Dair Farrah-Hockley, the Ops Officer, was leaving the Ops Room to find out what all the screaming and shouting was about.

Dair took me into the Ops Room and gave me a cup of tea, which helped to stem my flood of tears. Lovely man. Pat Wood, not so lovely.

Author's note:

John Reith the Adjutant had, I believe, two NDs with his pistol at the unloading bay at Springfield Road police station which was also Tac. HQ.

I managed to get everyone through the pipe range today to check zero their weapons.

There was some suspicious activity in the area of 4 Kashmir Rd. There was heavy dicking in operation, Dermott Perry was in a state of great agitation, in fact he was shitting himself. Mrs Rosebotham said 'hello boys, how are you all?' to a patrol – the first kind word she has ever said. Also some A2 and D2 PIRA were seen there. We think that either stuff was being moved or possibly some training or a lecture was in progress. By 0100 all was quiet.

RESTRICTED

ARMY CODE No. 71039

RULES OF ENGAGEMENT FOR PVC BATON ROUNDS

General
1. Baton rounds may be used to disperse a crowd whenever it is judged to be minimum and reasonable force in the circumstances.

2. THE ROUNDS must be fired at selected persons and not indiscriminately at the crowd. They should be aimed so that they strike the lower part of the target's body directly (ie without bouncing).

Additional Rules for the 25 Grain PVC Baton Round
3. The authority to use these rounds is delegated to the commander on the spot.

4. ROUNDS MUST NOT BE FIRED AT A RANGE OF LESS THAN 20 METRES EXCEPT WHEN THE SAFETY OF SOLDIERS OR OTHERS IS SERIOUSLY THREATENED.

5. The baton round was designed and produced to disperse crowds. It can also be used to prevent an escape from HM Prisons if it is, in the circumstances, still considered to constitute the use of minimum and reasonable force. If a prisoner can be apprehended by hand, the baton round must not be used.

RESTRICTED

RESTRICTED

Additional Rules for the 45 Grain PVC
Baton Round

6. The 45 grain PVC baton round is only
to be used in circumstances in which the 25
grain PVC round is ineffective. Rules 1 and 2
above apply to both types of round.

7. Authority to use the 45 grain PVC round
must be obtained from the brigade commander,
who may delegate this authority on specific
occasions.

8. The orders to fire the round are to be given
only by a commander not below platoon/troop
level at the scene of the incident, and he is
to control the fire throughout the engagement.

9. The round is to be fired only by a soldier
or soldiers who are specially selected by the
officer in charge, have been trained in its use,
and are aware of its characteristics.

10. In order to avoid any risk of confusion,
soldiers selected to fire the 45 grain PVC round
are not to be issued with any other type of
baton round.

11. The round is NEVER to be fired at ranges
less than 35m, or in circumstances in which
persons between the firer and the target are
within an angle of 30° either side of the line
of fire.

Revised December 1975

RESTRICTED

Rules of Engagement for the Baton Round (rubber bullet).
Army Code No. 71039, Ministry of Defence © Crown Copyright 1975.

Friday 25th February

On patrol 0100-0500.

Two lengths of det cord and a second world war respirator were found in a derelict in Kashmir Rd. Possibly a training place or factory. The finds were in good condition and had not been there for long.

Four buses were burnt out in the New Lodge and Cliftonville area.

A hoax bomb was planted in a van outside the RUC police station Tenant St, Felix towed it to some waste ground where it was declared an elaborate hoax. The UVF said that they laid it in protest over the RUC harassment of the Shankhill Rd black taxis. They claimed, quite rightly I think, that the Shankhill taxis were being purged but not the Falls taxis.

A 5-10 lb bomb exploded in an RC shop on the Crumlin Road. It was placed by two armed men who gave a warning, fired one round into the ceiling and ran off. It caused blast damage to twenty five meters and slightly injured two women.

A bomb hoax was phoned in, in an English accent to Hughes Bakery, possibly as a come-on. NFTR.

A warning has been issued to SF to look out in the Hawthorne, Earls Court and Cavendish St areas. Possibly with the intention of pulling troops into those areas to divert attention.

Search of 19 Benares St NTR.

Went to bed 0530, got up 1530. Good kip.

A quiet day for 2 PARA.

One RUC, Joseph Campbell, was shot, VSI in Cushendall, Co Antrim. Died later on.

One male killed in a stabbing in Sandy Row.

Nine mortar rounds were found in Tyrone. Bomb making kit found in Londonderry.

Two soldiers from the Queens were slightly injured in rioting in Turf Lodge. 2 x BR fired at fifty youths, windows and cars damaged, the usual!

An eight pound bomb was found in a car wired as a booby trap in Antrim. Neutralised later.

A grocer's shop was burnt out by two armed men in Newry.

Saturday 26th February

On patrol 0100-0500.

Found a woman outside 19 Clonard Gardens who seemed drunk. She said she'd been threatened and she showed me several rather vague signs inside her house that indicated threats. E.g. a noose and an upside down plug! She had OD'd on some tablets and I called for an ambulance to take her away.

Shots heard in the area of Clonard Monastery.

Chased a speeding car from there and caught it on the Falls by the Divis Flats. The driver was a Provo officer from Newtonhamilton. Nothing found.

At 0340 a civilianised RUC car containing two plain clothes RUC stopped at the traffic lights at Cambrai/Shankhill Rd junction. As it pulled up two masked men brandishing hand guns jumped out of the gloom, one on each side of the car. They said that this was a hijack and pointed their weapons into the car. The constable in the passenger seat promptly shot the man by his window. The man by the driver then shot the RUC driver. The RUC passenger then shot that gunman who was hit but ran off. One gunman was taken the RVH where he is VSI with GSW to the abdomen. The remaining gunman escaped leaving a trail of blood. A typical Irish incident. Lovely.

A 21 man patrol of N/K Regiment had to fire BRs to extricate themselves from a crowd of about forty. Not a very professional show, more aggression needed!

We have since heard that the wounded gunman has been captured, he is NSI in RVH.

A find was made of a rifle, 600 rounds and bomb making kit in Dungannon.

A car showroom was set on fire and burnt for five hours in the city centre.

Fifty to sixty taxis went on a protest drive through the city centre. No incidents.

Planned search NTR.

A man was arrested in the Clonard by Cpl Barber for having a microswitch and wire in his possession.

A red flare was seen in the sky in the Village area.

Sunday 27th February

A seventy year old businessman, Robert Mitchell, was shot and killed by gunmen in Newry, he was also a Justice of the Peace.

On watch 0130-0730.

A search of Carnlough Construction Co. Nothing found but a possible hide was discovered. It seemed old or temporary.

Gerry Adams, allegedly one time Belfast Brigade Commander PIRA who was recently released from the Maze has been seen on a number of occasions in Ballymurphy. It is not yet known what post he will take or whether he will stay low and act as an advisor.

2150, heard an explosion. Turned out to be a car bomb in York St, two people killed (James Cordner and Joseph Long, both UVF). First reports are an own goal. The bomb consisted of 5-10lbs of commercial gelignite equivalent and was placed in a car parked on Corporation St.

Ninety pounds of explosives were found in Dungannon as was 10 x .22 rifles, dets, TPUs and ammo. There have been a number of good finds there recently, probably the work of a good source.

An RC man was shot and killed whilst walking in the Ardoyne. Tit for tat we think. He was John Lee, ex UDR and ex-PARA.

Mrs Betty Williams of the Peace Movement said there would be a bombing 'doomsday' in the summer She also said that there were enough explosives to wipe out Belfast. Some peace movement, why doesn't she tell the authorities where it is then... fear of death?

RESTRICTED

Army Code No. 70772B

This card supersedes Army Code 70772A

Instructions by the Director of Operations for making Arrests in Northern Ireland

(Effective 8 August 1973)

PROCEDURE

1. These instructions are for the guidance of Commanders and troops when making arrests.

2. A soldier* may, under the Northern Ireland (Emergency Provisions) Act 1973, arrest any person, not below the age of 10 years, whom he suspects of committing, having committed or being about to commit any offence.

3. The soldier making the arrest must say "As a member of Her Majesty's Forces, I arrest you".

4. Arrested persons are to be handed over to the police or released as soon as possible. Persons not released as a result of screening must be handed over **as quickly as possible and must by law be so handed over or released within four hours.** Persons arrested by soldiers are to be handed over to an RMP Arrest Team, except that in very exceptional circumstances, and where there would otherwise be no option but to release them, they may be handed over directly to the RUC. In such a case an RMP Arrest Team is to be informed of the action taken as quickly as possible.

RESTRICTED

RESTRICTED

TREATMENT OF ARRESTED PERSONS

5. Soldiers should be firm in carrying out arrests, but physical force should be used only when the arrest cannot be made without it. In any case only such force as is reasonable in the circumstances may be used.

INFORMING RELATIVES

6. The soldier making the arrest is to leave the appropriate white card with any relative present at the time. This card contains guidance for relatives on how to obtain information about arrested persons.

7. Where a relative is not present and the person arrested requests that a relative be informed, the RUC to whom that person is handed over by the RMP Arrest Team, are to be asked to comply with this request.

8. Where a juvenile (ie a person between 10 and 17 years of age) is arrested, the unit making the arrest is to ensure that the parent or guardian is informed why the juvenile is being arrested and where he is being held.

---

* Throughout these instructions the word soldier is to be taken to include members of the Royal Navy, Royal Marines and Royal Air Force, including womens services, as well as members of the Army.

August 1973

RESTRICTED Dd0734106/75N.W.Ltd.

Army Code No. 70722B, Ministry of Defence © Crown Copyright 1973.

Monday 28th February

The bomb that exploded last night has been confirmed as an own goal. Two men, identified this afternoon, were carrying a duffel bag from a car when it went off. Both were Protestants on the way to hit a club or bar. It took the SF some time to assemble the bodies as arms, legs and other bits and pieces were scattered all over Corporation St.

A man was shot three times in the Ardoyne and was DOA at hospital. He lived at Mountainview Gardens and was later confirmed as a former member of The Parachute Regiment, John Lee: see yesterday's report.

Ninety two pounds of Co-op mix were found in Dungannon, the source there is very keen.

An n/k soldier was jailed for five years for manslaughter having killed someone two years ago whilst on duty. NFI.

Took a pig load of Toms to Hollywood to go swimming but when we got there the pool wasn't available until 1600 so that was a waste of time. Better homework needed lads. Spent the time supping beers and watching the Gordon Highlanders playing the Grenadier Guards at football. Met Capt Ian Chant-Semphill who is their Adjutant, we were at school together in the '60's.

The following figures have been released for the period of <u>two weeks</u> ending on 22nd February 1977:

People charged:

Murder	4
Firearms offences	12
Explosives offences	4
Attempted murder	1
Armed robbery	2
Miscellaneous	2

Plus 97 arrests made by the Army in connection with finds.

Finds:

Catholic weapons   9

Protestant weapons   5

Weapon types   3 x MG, 1 x SG, 5 x rifles, 5 x pistols.

Explosives   132 lbs.

Total shootings:	Belfast	Londonderry	Rural	
	28	6	15	(49 total)
Contacts with SF	16	4	8	(28 total)
Explosions	6	2	9	(17 total)
Devices neutralised	4	5	6	(15 total)

RESTRICTED

a. The process should be repeated until the whole area is cleared. (ECM cover is provided by ATO).

DERELICTS

10. Rather than risk lives, derelicts, and sometimes even houses, should be destroyed by the ATO using a controlled explosion or burning, taking into account surrounding property.

11. Derelicts should be destroyed, in accordance with paragraph 10, even when a find of arms or other terrorist devices is suspected, particularly when there is any intelligence that explosives or booby traps are present.

12. Permission to destroy derelicts is to be obtained from Bde. HQ, as there may be overriding intelligence grounds to 'stake-out' the derelict rather than destroy it.

REMEMBER!

TIME AND PROPERTY MEAN NOTHING:
LIVES MEAN EVERYTHING

RESTRICTED

Guidelines for Dealing with Terrorist Ambush Bombs and Booby Traps

WARNING

1. NEVER touch a suspicious object or approach the site of a suspect explosive device. "STAKE-OUT" (remembering the range of radio controlled devices), secure and search all vantage points.

2. Most incidents begin with an explosion, or the SF finding, or being informed of, a bomb, an attractive find or a possible capture.

3. DO NOT RISK LIFE to save property or time.

INITIAL ASSESSMENT

4. Carefully assess and check the reliability of the information, suspect a lure and decide whether the SF must react immediately or whether they can delay. Remember, once you decide to react, the initiative passes into your hands.

IMMEDIATE REACTION OPERATION

5. If the SF must react immediately, then proceed with caution as follows:
   a. Set up Incident Control Point.
   b. Call for ATO. Consider need for sniffer and tracker dogs and RE search party.

Guidelines for Dealing with Terrorist Ambush Bombs and Booby Traps
Ministry of Defence © Crown Copyright 1975.

Tuesday 1ˢᵗ March

During the night a man jumped from the second floor of Springfield Rd RUC, he was being questioned at the time. Luckily he landed on a car parked in the yard and was taken to hospital where he is VSI.

Five buses were burnt in Ballymena.

The UVF has claimed that both people killed in last night's bomb were members of an 'active service unit' on duty. One was a Captain and one a volunteer. What a price to pay for a negligent discharge!

Another Prot businessman was shot, VSI, whilst walking to work in Portadown.

Troops found 220 lbs of Anfo (Ammonium nitrate and fuel oil, very unstable homemade explosives, this has caused of a lot of own goals) and 20 lbs of Co-op during a planned search in Londonderry.

The man who jumped from the police station was being questioned in connection with Claymores found in the Ballymurphy. At his house were found photocopies of maps, on which were marked the locations of various devices found by Sp Coy. It was during questioning by RUC CID that he took off and dived head first from the third storey, landing on a civvy car and damaging it. His chances of recovery are put at 50/50 and if he does recover will be charged in connection with the finds.

A man was shot twice in the knee in A Coy's area.

A very good book on small arms was found during a planned search. The page on the Winchester Savage being particularly well thumbed.

There was a small demo outside Springfield RUC.

A report says that the standard of Army patrols has gone down and this increases the likelihood of a hit. This was highlighted as being in the Springfield Rd area.

Two awards for compensation have been made, one for a child blinded by a BR, £60,000 and one to a child injured by a booby trap at £85,000. It makes us feel good to know that a soldier's wife will get £5,000 on his death or as in one recent case nothing as they had only been married for a few months. It's good to feel wanted.

Wednesday 2nd March

Yet another businessman, Donald Robinson has been killed by PIRA. This one was shot in his office on the University Road.

Two incendiaries went off in an hotel in Newry but caused little damage. A third was defused.

A car bomb was found in the city centre, a package with wires sticking out was seen in the back. ATO attended.

On patrol 0900-1300.

Took two cars to Broadway to be searched at the CVSC at Blairs Yard. RMP escorted.

A police reservist had a lucky escape in Co Tyrone. His dog started scratching at the empty fireplace in his house. Upon investigation he found a ten pound bomb that had been lowered down the chimney. It was safely neutralised.

A .303 Lee Enfield was found in a culvert with some ammunition in Lurgan.

L/Cpl Gibbins found some subversive literature at 6 McQuillan St. They included a handbook on small arms, the 'Poor Man's James Bond' and a couple of vaguely revolutionary books. The dog also indicated but nothing was found. The house was an occupied derelict.

11 x .223 empty cases were found in the Rodney St James area of A Coy's patch. It is thought that they were used when a civvy Land Rover was shot up yesterday and a man was hit in the legs. It was a grey LR van so probably mistaken for an RUC one.

There was a bomb scare at the VW firm in North Howard Street. (*A portent of events to come*).

A man was arrested for spitting at Sgt MacNaughton, he was later let off with a warning by the RUC. I doubt that we would have been treated so leniently if one of us lost his rag! Hey ho!

Thursday 3rd March

Two bombs exploded in the city, both outside houses of businessmen, no cas.

Shots fired at an RUC on the Crumlin Rd, he was hit in the hand.

Lord Faulkner, former prime minister of NI was killed in a riding accident.

Cpl Blowers saw a figure crawling along the roof of the Hong Kong Café on Springfield R. FUNTR, possibly a burglar.

A photocopy of a PIRA explosives manual was available for reading. It had been handwritten in very bad English and really was a fools guide to bomb making. It contained advice such as: 'Don't smoke when making bombs as the whole lot can go up.' Also child like drawings of 'Brit Jeeps' being blown up together with 'BOOMS and KERRASK!' It did contain sufficient information to make a basic bomb, however ATO assured us that anyone following these instructions would be very lucky not to get himself killed.

On patrol 0900-1300. Spent most of the time ferrying people to and from Tac HQ. We found a tea stop in Northumberland St, the first of the tour.

We went to Blairs Yard to pick up a WRAC for a search. When we arrived they were all in bed and we were invited to wait in their rest room. During this time we were subjected to the horrible sight of a semi naked fat WRAC. The door had been opened and there was a mass of screaming female flesh being leered at by a patrol of Paratroopers.

Friday 4th March

On patrol 0900-1300.

Spent a lot of time ferrying people to 219 and back.

On watch 1730-2130. A few shots were heard in the area of the graveyard.

Another businessman was shot and killed today. This one was in Coalisland. PIRA claimed responsibility. Being a businessman of any repute is becoming distinctly unhealthy, there must be many frightened people. They do provide a good, safe and easy targets for PIRA with little chance of being caught or shot at. Rory O'Kelly, killed by PIRA.

Two bombs exploded inside the segments of the city causing structural damage to a pub and a ladies lavatory. No cas.

A bomb did minor damage to a supermarket in Londonderry.

Bomb scare at Wilkes Engineering in First St. We went up to investigate, did a brief search and RUC declared the area clear. The employees didn't seem bothered and used it as an excuse for a smoke break.

The man shot in Coalisland was a Crown Prosecutor. PIRA say they will kill lawyers.

Felix defused a 60lb bomb on the Antrim Rd, it was soaked in petrol.

Saturday 5th March

On watch 0730-1230.

Search of waste ground at the back of McQuillan St was neg. A car was taken to the vehicle search centre, otherwise all quiet.

Had a snooze in the afternoon when England beat Wales.

On watch 1730-2130.

A few shots were heard in the Whiterock.

A grey van with GO painted on the side and smelling of marzipan avoided a B Coy VCP, a Rat Trap was put out with no results.

Heard on the Battalion Net:

"Hello 0 this is R41B, I am approaching your area with Nite-sun, do you have any tasks for me? Over."

"0, you are difficult, radio check, over."

"R41B OK, over."

"0, You are unworkable, I suggest that you return to base and change your batteries, over."

R41B ignored this assuming that the Regimental Signals Officer, Lt. Colin Gordon was switched off. As we all knew R41B was a helicopter.

There was a small shoot out between gunmen and the RUC on the Antrim Rd, seven shots were fired from a passing car, RUC returned fire, no cas.

A man died as a result of a pub brawl in Sandy Row. Not believed to be sectarian.

1 x .3006 Garrand found in the Markets.

1 x SLR and 17 x 7.62 found in New Lodge. Both in back garden outhouses so the owner can't be held responsible.

Sunday 6th March

On watch 0730-1230.

A report in the Sunday Telegraph stated that terrorists were salvaging explosives from the wreck of HMS Drake. She sank in 1917 after being torpedoed and was towed to shallow water off Rathlin Island, Co Antrim. Apparently the explosives were in quite good condition. Some terrorists captured have been found to have traces of picric acid on their skin. This would be present in old decomposing WW1 explosives particularly due to a change in temperature following removal from cool sea to warm air. The wreck has since been cleared by Royal Navy divers.

A Mr McDonald of 3PIRA was caught with certain documents and articles that linked him to the find last month in Liverpool of a bomb factory. He is known to be the explosives officer of 3PIRA.

The Newry Device is on the loose again. It is a mercury or ball bearing tilt switch used to booby trap almost anything.

A march from Whiterock to Castle St is planned for this pm. It is an illegal march in aid of the political status kick. The march ended up with about 250-300 including a couple of bands. At King/Castle St they were addressed by a hog who spoke for about ten minutes then the marchers dispersed. Some marching back up the Falls. NFTR.

There was a gun battle between police and gunmen in Co. Armagh, no cas and the gunmen fled across the border. RUC fired 109 x 9mm.

A detonator exploded in the face of an eleven year old boy who found it in a stream. NSI.

A bomb exploded in a sewer in Londonderry, possibly an ND, no cas.

A .303 rifle was found in Armagh.

108 rounds of assorted ammo were found in a derelict in the Prot Bone.

Monday 7th March. OUR BOMB and The Egg Banjo Battle.

A man was killed when gunmen shot him through the front door of his house in Craigavon, Armagh.

A member of the UDR was shot dead on his farm and his body was dumped on a border crossing. (Poss Pte J Reid UDR)

A UDR man is VSI as he was shot at work in Twinbrook. Two others with him are NSI.

A youth was tarred and feathered in the Lower Falls.

On watch 0730-1230, very quiet.

On patrol 1645-1845. All very quiet until the end of the patrol. We had stopped some people and I was doing a P check so told L/Cpl Camp to go through me and carry on back to base. We were moving down the Falls with Tom Camp's brick of four men ahead of me by about 30 metres. He turned left into North Howard Street and we stopped just by the corner by the swimming baths. As we moved forward a few seconds later there was a large explosion. The first thing I saw was a burst of flame and then the blast hit followed by smoke, shrapnel and the sound of falling glass from the swimming bath windows.

We cocked our weapons, I put in the radio call, "Hello G4 this is G41L, contact, North Howard Street, wait out," and ran forward into NHSt where visibility was almost zero and bits and pieces were still falling out of the sky. Pte Scouse Magerison *(Later wounded at Goose Green)* was shouting 'fucking bastards!'

My first reaction was to ensure there was no follow up shooting and then to check for our own casualties. I was sure that we would find bits and pieces of L/Cpl Camps's patrol lying all over the place. As I couldn't see anything due to smoke, dust and dusk I called him up on the radio and thank God he answered rather shakily that they were all NSI. In fact Pte Reid had sustained a broken leg and lacerations. Tom Camp and Pte Donkin, I think, picked him up and carried him the short distance to our front sangar. His section had all been blown over and were cut and bruised but otherwise OK. Pte Reid and L/Cpl Jones were given first aid then transported by Saracen to the Musgrave Park Hospital where they are NSI.

We cordoned off the Falls Rd and surrounding area and waited until ATO etc. turned up. We will have to wait for forensic results to find out if it was command detonated or whether we tripped it. I hope not.

We hung around outside for ages before being called back in, I allowed the Toms to have secret ciggies and I cadged a drag or two myself. Press turned up but I just told them to move on or go to Tac for the official version. It was frustrating not to have a target or two to let rip at.

The bomb was in a VW van that had been hijacked at 1700, so not long before, on the Falls, Springfield junction. NHSt is always filled with VWs being repaired at the Isaac Agnews workshops, so the one that went up was not suspicious nor was there sufficient time for SF to be notified of the hijacking. The bomb was not really sophisticated as it appears that it hadn't been laced with shipyard confetti, unusual, quite possibly it was a hurried job.

In addition a man sitting in his house on the street was injured by debris and was treated by us and taken to hospital, NSI.

Our men were not in a friendly mood. I retired to the mess after a debrief and scoff to take in a little Bushmills! (No one asked us how we were, nowadays we'd have had counselling! And we didn't get a mention in Pegasus Notes.)

Pte Keith Donkin's recollections:

Walking down the road before the bomb went off, I remember looking into a window and seeing a guy working at a bench, then looking into the car which had the bomb in and saying to myself, there's something not right.

I walked past the car level with a van, then the bomb went off. The van took the hit and I was thrown over the van into the middle of the road. Our reaction was to cock our weapons, we couldn't see a thing.

Later that night CSM Duncan sent for me in the Op Room. He said, you're staying here for a few hours so we can look after you. About an hour later he said, go and get me an egg banjo. I came back give him the egg banjo, he bit into it and the egg went all down his jumper. He told me fuck off to bed. Two days later me and Tom were back on the streets.

Pte David Smith's recollections:

I do remember that after we got back in base after the bomb in NHS and being out there in the cold for so long even with a sneaky smoke (thanks for that), when we went to the cook house for some scran Scouse Mage said if they offer us egg banjos, the lazy crap hat bastards, I will kill them. Oh yeah, the cook offered us egg banjos. Scouse chased him around the cook house determined to beat the fuck out of him and caught him. We ate steak and chips that night.

At some other time we were doing the guard duty at the telephone exchange, me and Scouse had a big fall-out with Tom Camp. Scouse ended up hitting him, the two of them scrapping all over the place. Tom beat the shit out of him. I was in Tom's section, but because of the major fall-out I swapped places with Jock Reid; he should have been with you that day, not me, he got what I should have. That was defo double good luck for me, but felt so guilty about it and sometimes when I think back I still do. Keep wondering what he's doing now, and you were totally right now, it's PTSD, we were soldiers and just had to get on with the job, and we did.

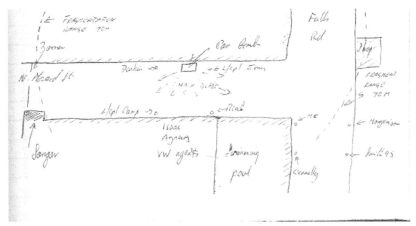

A drawing I made just after the explosion.

The bomb site.

Looking towards North Howard Street main gate
Sangar from the Falls Rd.

Extract from Brigade SITREP.

Tuesday 8th March

SOCO has confirmed that the bomb was a radio controlled device, the charge was about 20-30lbs of Anfo and was placed in the back of a VW van.

The bombers had relied on the van to provide shrapnel, had they added some the outcome could have been very different.

I visited L/Cpl Jones and Pte Reid in hospital. Jonesy is OK, with a couple of cuts on his legs and is just being kept in for observation. Reid has his left leg broken and is quite badly lacerated. They have pulled several lumps of shrapnel out of it. His DMS boots are shredded. His right foot has also received minor injuries. He will be in hospital for a few weeks to come. Pte Donkin was completely unmarked, They were all rather battered as they got blown down the street. Their only memories of the explosion are a huge bang and all the windows jumping out at them, then being thrown over and finally the sounds of bits and pieces falling out of the sky.

An explosion in Crossmaglen, one soldier slightly hurt.

A youth was shot in the neck in the area of the Malone Rd, NSI.

An RUC was shot in the arm on the Crumlin Rd near Flax St, NSI. *Where we were in 1975.* 6 x 5.56 fired, 2 x 7.62 returned.

On patrol 1415-1615 and again 2130-2345, very quiet, no baddies about. We were quite alert following yesterday's excitement. All searches negative apart from an empty BR case.

Wednesday 9th March

It has struck me that as we were about to move back to base on Monday evening, L/Cpl Camp came up on the radio and said that as he was nearer the base than I was could he lead his brick in along the Falls. It was usual for me to lead the way in but because of our location ten minutes before the end of the patrol I decided that he should go in first. Had our patrol been the same as usual it would have been my C/S that got blasted. L/Cpl Camp pointed this out to me with some amusement later on!

On patrol 1400-1555, NTR.

The SAS patrol arrested last year for straying over the border were acquitted of the charge of having weapons with intent. They were fined £100 each for not having firearms certificates! The government is paying the fines.

On patrol 1900-2100. Area deserted. There is a definite lack of known baddies and heavies about, whether this is because they don't want to get buggered about by us we don't know.

Its known that PIRA took delivery of thirteen sets of radio control units, having used one it is confirmed that twelve are still in circulation in Belfast.

A .303 Lee Enfield was found in the Markets during the follow up to yesterday's shooting on the Crumlin Rd.

A man was shot in the neck in Cliftonville and is VSI.

A search of the derelicts in Cupar St was negative.

The IO reckons that he knows who was responsible for the bomb – can he do anything about it? It is thought that the only connection that C2 PIRA had was to organise the hijacking of the van. This seems most likely according to IO.

L/Cpl Jones was discharged from hospital, Reid will be sent back home once he is fit to be moved.

A member of the UDR was shot dead on his farm and his body was dumped on a border crossing.

Call Sign G41L

L/Cpl Mick 'Gibbo' Gibbins, on the right 'carried his relationship a stage further' with the WRAC! Steve Prior KIA at Goose Green, 'Billy' Connelly, Adams, Atkinson, Smith 28, Sharpe, Self, L/ Cpl Gibbins, NK WRAC.

The Story of Private Adams. Recalled by Nick O'Connor:

It was Pte Adams MA. He went to Gordonstoun. Nice bloke. I knew his background. How, I have no idea.

Some years later in Berlin, the now Cpl Adams, was in the Intelligence Section.

When Prince Charles was inspecting the troops in Brooke Barracks he stopped in front of Adams and said, 'Good Lord, Pogo,' or similar, 'what are you doing here?'

'I'm a paratrooper, sir,' said Adams.

'Well, yes, I can see that, Pogo,' said HRH, 'but I thought you went to university.'

'I did, sir.'

'Yes, well... well done.' And off toddled HRH to meet Susan George.

Well. That's another story. And that is a tale that both you and I can tell. Dear God. Great days.

Michael Emberson tells another, later story concerning Pte Adams:

I also remember Adam's (Chris?) as a nice guy – bit of a fish out of water – always dressed off duty as (his words) 'the duty vet' in a tweed jacket with leather elbow patches, check shirt, knitted tie and cavalry twill trousers.

He had so he told me (and I have no reason to disbelieve him) been a lighthouse keeper in Scotland before joining up – something he gave up because the 'loneliness was getting to me'.

Short, happy-go-lucky character – bit of an oddball – but then again 2 PARA had plenty of them!

I once passed the guardroom with him when the Provost Sgt (Moriaty – evil twat) pulled him up for something and asked him his name. 'Adams, Sarn't.'

'From the family of the same name I presume, you little cunt,' says Moriaty!

The strong bonds of the Airborne brotherhood then required me to slink away stage right so I'm not sure how it ended – probably a show parade.

Thursday 10th March

Search was NTR.

Went to Echelon and signed for £998 for repayment of telephone money – pity we didn't get ambushed, I'm sure it would have been 'lost'!

Very heavy rain and wind, a miserable day.

A bomb attack was made on the house of an RUC reservist. He was out.

An RUC reservist was shot on his farm in Co. Fermanagh by three gunmen, he was hit several times but is NSI.

An eighteen year old boy, Norman Sharkie, was killed by PIRA gunmen when he surprised them planting bombs in York St, the bombs subsequently detonated destroying a showroom.

1 x HV fired at 1 Queens by Norglen roundabout, no cas FUNTR.

A man was shot with a shotgun in New Lodge. DOA.

A D&D Op saw a woman limping along the Antrim Rd. She was stopped by a foot patrol who found a sawn off shotgun under her skirts.

It is known who was behind our car bomb on Monday. He is being allowed to stay free for two reasons. Firstly, they want to get more evidence against him and secondly so that he can be followed to see if he will lead us to more important contacts etc. The prime targets are the radio control experts and their sources.

The Clonard touts have been very forthcoming ref this incident so we are told.

A warehouse was destroyed by fire following a couple of small explosions, down by the docks somewhere.

A youth was kneecapped on the Shankhill Rd, NSI. He was shot twice with a .22, also another kneecapping in Londonderry.

Friday 11th March

On watch 0130-0730.

Suspect car found in Clonard St/Dunmore St, the lights were on and it had been abandoned. A car check told us that it had been stolen in Larne and had been involved in a hit and run. Felix was tasked and fired a few shots into it without result so he carried out three controlled explosions of varying sizes which reduced the car to a wreck. It caught fire and burnt out, a pity really as it was a brand new Ford Capri.

2 Royal Anglian Regt advance party arrived.

A source has said that PIRA are intending to have another go at NHSt with a bomb. Good luck Anglians!

A Tom from Sp Coy was shot in the side on the Whiterock/ Glenalina Rd junction. The round passed straight through him, he is NSI. Lucky chap. The round was fired from the Turf Lodge. A and Sp Coys must be getting fed up from being fired at from the craphats' areas. FU found an Armalite and a pistol.

A bomb attack in Londonderry on an SF base.

A two lb device surrounded by five gallons of petrol was defused in the Falls Rd bus station.

A small bomb slightly damaged a house in the Ballysillan.

Went to visit Pte Reid in MPH. He's very perky and is well on the way to recovery. It will be about three weeks before he is out of plaster and is due to be casevaced home on Wednesday. He says he's having his bum washed by the nurses and how difficult it is to shit in bed. Several of the Toms seem quite jealous of his wounds! If he'd been American he'd have a Purple Heart.

A bomb badly damaged a car showroom in the Antrim Rd, no cas.

Three incendiary devices were found and defused in Londonderry.

Two small bombs exploded under two cars on the Shankhill, no cas.

Ref the Sp Coy shooting. FUIHP (follow up in hot pursuit) 4 x pistols, 1 x M16, a silencer and 200+ rounds were found in Glenisla Rd.

Saturday 12th March

PIRA have claimed responsibility for our bomb on NHSt and the shooting yesterday. Must be pissed off losing an M16.

In yesterday's follow up Sp Coy also made three arrests in connection with their finds. Also found was a .3008 Remington hunting rifle.

It is sourced that a new ASU (active service unit) has been formed in the Ballymurphy. Their intention is to avenge the incident when Rooney fell out of the Springfield Rd station window. It is believed that Moyner is one of the group. It's likely they will try a snipe either against us or RUC.

On watch 0100-0730, nothing at all happened.

Slept through until 1545.

The Royal Anglians are gradually settling in. No one thinks very much of them, we look forward with relish to see how they are received once we depart. The officer who I am showing around and briefing is particularly pompous. Lots of "*Oh I know it well, yes, yes, yes, we don't need to bother with that, done it all before etc.*" Fucking idiot.

A bomb exploded under a car by the Crumlin Rd Gaol, the car belonged to a prison warder. This was the third attempt against warders in the last twenty four hours.

Sunday 13th March

On watch 0130-0730. NTR.

Planned search of Hughes Bakery 1000-1600 revealed:

1 x Webley automatic pistol.
5 x 5.56 rounds.
105 x .22 long rounds.
1 x NK magazine.
A quantity of documents of Int interest.
A snipe position being prepared in the front of the building.

Two women have been charged in connection with the weapons found by Sp Coy, the house was described on the house card as having a history of friendliness and cooperation.

B Coy have, for the past three weeks, been manning covert Ops on the Falls overlooking pubs. They have established among other things that PIRA & IRSP are working together. They also established that standing on plaster in a loft will result in a Tom falling through into the shop below and thoroughly compromising the OP!

Gerry Adams has, allegedly, stood down C2 & D2 PIRA pending reorganisation.

It's known that Bendo McKee pressed the tit on our car bomb. B Coy searched 1A Lower Clonard St acting on a tip off before the bomb exploded. It is thought that they missed it by about five minutes. The fact that it was made from Anfo suggests a shortage of co-op mix, Anfo being a lower grade explosive.

Author's Note: Bendo was imprisoned in 1981 and died I think in the 1990s.

Between 29/01/77 and now 2 PARA has recovered twenty three stolen vehicles, not bad.

It costs locals between £50-£100 to get their names on the housing waiting list. *(£300-£600 in today's money.)* This goes to PIRA as the Clonard Housing Association is PIRA run.

It is believed that 'quite a lot' of PIRA are becoming disenchanted with the 'struggle' and would like to leave. Easier said than done.

Albert Allen was given an IRA reprimand for failing to carry out a bombing run last month. His excuse was that patrol activity was too high for him to guarantee success.

An eighteen year old RUC constable, William Brown, was shot and killed in an ambush in Co. Fermanagh. In the FU an Army patrol also came under fire but there were no cas. He was the 100th RUC member to have been killed in the Troubles. 108 rounds returned, NHC.

There have been a series of small explosions in the Ballygomartin and Silverstream areas of Belfast no cas reported.

About 20 shots were fired at a former UDR man in Dungannon, hits to head and hand but NSI.

The rounds fired at the Tom from Sp Coy a few days ago were 5.56mm. 3 x 5.56 fired, 4 x 7.62 returned. The round went through the flak jacket and hit the side buckle on his OG trousers which cut and bruised him. The spent head was removed from his FJ.

A black taxi containing a hoax bomb was found in Clonard St/Falls.

After Felix destroyed it, it was declared a hoax. He he! Theory is that it was a diversion.

A .303 rifle was found in Portadown.

A number of NK rounds were fired at an Army patrol in Londonderry. No cas.

Monday 14th March

On patrol 0900-1300.

0400 — All known PIRA leaders in the Bn TAOR were lifted and taken to RUC Castlreagh for a beasting! This is to scotch any last minute attempt they may make against us. Hopefully without leaders plans will be harder to implement.

We lifted Richard Rosebotham, William Kelly and Gerard Bradley. Saw Dermott Perry, he looked very unhappy.

I think that we may have come under fire at a VCP on the upper Springfield Rd by the old garage site. I heard a heavy flat crack which was probably an HV but we heard no 'thump' or strike. No cas, NFTR. Maybe luck shines on us. Didn't put in a contact report.

Four small bombs exploded in the city segments badly damaging them this morning.

After a robbery in the Stirling Hotel on the Antrim Rd a bomb, placed by the robbers did moderate damage. No cas.

A British businessman, James Nicholson, was shot and killed by PIRA on Kennedy Way, Andersonstown, his driver was also hit and is VSI. Poor sod was on a one day visit to Belfast, sounds like a tip off.

PIRA has warned all civvies to keep away from SF bases, patrols and SF vehicles. The beginnings of yet another campaign? Yawn.

Feeling is running high within the RUC over the 'Tonight' TV programme ten days ago when people testified that they had been tortured by the RUC. They feel that this will kick off a new 'hate the RUC' campaign that resulted in the death of a young policeman yesterday.

The advance party to Aldershot left today. Everyone is packing kit and getting happy about returning home, real end of term stuff. It is vital that we survive the next thirty six hours without going soft and presenting an easy target. Let's keep our fingers crossed and put our trust in God and the power of a 7.62 round.

Belfast, a typical scene. Taken on my recce in a Sioux helicopter.

A small march.

VCP on the Falls Rd.

Falls Road.

Tuesday 15th March

On patrol 0900-1300.

Much of the time was spent ferrying people from one place to another, as well as showing the Anglians the area. Visited Moyard to see Sp Coy.

The CO got very upset when he found us stopped on the Shankhill Rd. Keith Shard wanted to buy a watch for his child so we stopped. He, the CO seemed unreasonably excited about it especially as we'd told NHSt where we were.

Rain and wind. Again.

1 UDR soldier, Pte D McQuillan, was shot and killed on the way to work in Macharafelt, his companion is VSI. He was the 70th UDR to die.

Another UDR was wounded, VSI in a similar attack.

And another UDR wounded NSI in Coalisland.

An Armalite rifle and 24 assorted rounds were found in the Old Park.

A UDR soldier posted as lost has been found and is being charged with the killing of a soldier from the Royal Hampshire Regiment in 1975.

Two more UDR men were shot at in Portadown, all shots missed and no fire was returned.

A Bardie lamp lost by the Engineers during the recent search of Hughes Bakery was found by a worker there. It was handed to Ben, the OC who put it on some open ground and tasked Felix who fired some shots at it and declared it safe and not boobied. Better safe than sorry. The last one that was found by CSM Anderson in 1975 had four ounces of PE inside and was set to go off when the torch was turned on. He couldn't get it to work so opened it up and there was the PE. We are told he went very white and wobbly.

Tonight we got the good news that the LSL (Landing Ship Logistics) has not yet sailed from Liverpool. Instead of sailing at 1130 it will leave at 2100, arriving here at about 2359. We'll be about four hours late getting into Aldershot.

A Saracen AFV, at Ballymurphy I think.

A Saracen after a paint job by the locals.

Wednesday 16th March. Tour ends at 2000hrs.

On patrol 0900-1300.

Sunny day, many people out and about shopping. Spent the patrol doing VCPs. NTR.

There was a minor traffic accident on Springfield/Forfar St, no cas.

There was an attempted hijacking on the Falls and a robbery at the post office.

Someone tried to slam the door at the Kash for Kesh shop in the face of L/Cpl Gibbins, the door was booted open and laid out the offender.

Some locals said they were surprised that we were still here.

2000 – the tour officially ended.

Our armed escort to the docks consisted of two Pioneers, one of whom had a foresight protector on his SLR thereby rendering the sights useless. He was re-educated.

Without any fuss we embarked upon LSL Sir Bedivere at 2130 and had a few beers.

By 2230 the entire battalion was onboard.

At 2235 the entire battalion was told to disembark onto the quay for the CO's farewell talk.

We sailed at about midnight, arriving in Liverpool at 1330. Oh the joy of lining up on Liverpool docks to get your 'credits' from the Paymaster.

The train journey went well enough and having handed in kit and weapons everyone was away from Montgomery Lines, Aldershot by 2230 Thursday 17th March.

I cadged a lift home with Maj Harvey to our married quarter in Church Crookham were I was greeted at the front door by Fhiona who asked where I'd been. "Belfast," I said.

PART 3

SLANG, TERMINOLOGY ABBREVIATIONS

- ANFO   Homemade explosives, ammonium nitrate and fuel oil.
- ATO   Ammunition technical officer. Bomb disposal.
- BR   Baton round (rubber/PVC).
- C/S   Call sign, i.e. a unit or sub unit identifier. Rather than CS gas.
- Cat   Catholic
- CATO   Chief ATO.
- Co-op   Homemade explosives, strongly smelling of marzipan.
- Colour man   CQMS (Colour Sgt.)
- Come-on   PIRA lure to SF for a bomb or snipe.
- Contact   When SF come under fire or bomb.
- Crack   The sound made by a HV bullet as it goes past you.
- Crap crusher   Night foot patrol.
- Craphat   Any Non-PARA soldier.
- Dicking   Early warning lookouts by junior IRA usually.
- DIFS   Department of Industrial and Forensic Science.

- DOA — Dead on arrival.
- Frangex — Commercial explosives for blasting.
- FUNTR — Follow up nothing to report.
- Hijack corner — Springfield Rd/Falls Rd junction, aptly named.
- Hog — Local lady with whom you would not form a relationship.
- HV — High velocity, supersonic round.
- IED — Improvised explosive device.
- IWS — Individual weapons site. (Starlight/Image intensifier)
- LV — Low velocity as in shots, sub sonic.
- Mobile flower show — Funeral.
- MPH — Musgrave Park Hospital.
- N(F)TR — Nothing (further) to report.
- ND — Negligent discharge, as in of one's personal weapon.
- NHC — No hits claimed.
- NIRT — NI reinforcement training.
- NITAT — NI Training and Advisory Team.
- NSI — Not seriously ill.
- OP — Observation post.
- Own goal — Someone who blows themselves up by mistake.
- Pig — Humber 1 ton armoured vehicle, as it looks and drives like a pig.
- Playboy — Immediate standby section.
- Prot — Protestant.
- Rat Trap — VCP imposed citywide for 10 mins for a specific vehicle.
- Rubber dick — Baton round.
- RUC — Royal Ulster Constabulary. *Post-Good Friday renamed PSNI.*

- RVH — Royal Victoria Hospital.
- Saracen — Six-wheeled armoured personnel carrier.
- SB — Special branch. (RUC)
- SF — Security forces.
- SFNI — Security forces not involved.
- Shipyard confetti — Shrapnel, nuts, bolts, nails etc.
- SIB — Special investigation branch, Royal Military Police.
- SLR — Self-loading rifle, as issued to us.
- SOCO — Scene of crime officer.
- SOP — Standard operating procedure.
- Squirrels — Intelligence section.
- Stickies — Official IRA.
- SUIT — Sight Unit, Infantry, Trilux.
- Taigs — Protestant slang for Catholics
- TAC — Tactical headquarters, Springfield Rd police station.
- Thump — The sound of the gun shot, follows the crack.
- Tom — Private soldier in The Parachute Regiment.
- Tout — Informer. A dangerous job!
- UDR — Ulster Defence Regiment
- VCP — Vehicle check point.
- VSI — Very seriously ill.
- Wog shop — Canteen run by Indians/Pakis.
  Not very PC now but that's how it was.

PART 4

APPOINTMENT TITLES

Big Bull   Assistant chief constable, Belfast.
Brimstone   Padre.
Coffee pot   Female RMP.
Felix   ATO.
Greenfinch   UDR female.
Groundhog   Tracker dog.
Hush Puppy   SIB.
Kestrel   Ops officer.
Moonbeam   Chief of Staff.
Mushroom   Watch keeper.
Neptune   Water cannon.
Nite Sun   Airborne searchlight, usually on a helicopter.
Nutcracker   Bomb intelligence team.
Pointer   RMP evidence team.
Prophet   Unit press officer.
Ruckbag   RUC female.
Rucksack   RUC.
Scooby (doo)   Medium-wheeled tractor. (Royal Engineers)
Snapper   Watch dog.
Starlight   Medic/Reg Medical Officer.
Top Cat   CATO.
Wagtail   Search dog, arms or explosives.

PART 5

NORTHERN IRISH PARTIES AND ORGANISATIONS

CNB	Female branch of PIRA. Cumann na mBan
DOW	Down Orange Welfare. Prot.
FIANNA	Junior branch of PIRA.
IRSP	Irish Republican and Socialist Party. Cat.
NICRA	Northern Ireland Civil Rights Association. Mainly Cat.
OIRA	Official Irish Republican Army. Cat
OV	Orange Volunteers. Prot.
PD	People's Democracy, similar to NICRA.
PIRA	Provisional IRA. Cat
Republican Clubs.	OIRA front. Cat.
RHC	Red Hand Commandos. Prot.
Sinn Fein	Political wing of IRA. Cat.
TARA	Republican Organisation of Queers. Cat. *LBGT in today's PC parlance.*
UAC	Ulster Army Council. Prot.
UDA	Ulster Defence Association. Prot.
UFF	Ulster Freedom Fighters. Prot.
UVF	Ulster Volunteer Force. Prot.
UWC	Ulster Workers Council. Prot.
YCV	Young Citizens Volunteers. Prot, branch of UVF.

PART 6

RANDOM NOTES AND GOSSIP FROM MY DAILY ORDERS GROUP LOG AND OTHER UNNAMED SOURCES

- P checks – get spelling correct, call in to 0 then, not later.
- Mobiles can have a tea break every two hours. One man to collect.
- Mobiles should not drive continuously, beware of following each other.
- Make sure you know how to use DIFS bags.
- Sentries to wear cam cream and helmets. No netting or scrim on helmets.
- If assaulted the arresting Tom is the primary witness.
- Mobiles can go to the wog shop.
- Tea and butties 0200-0600, return containers and clean up.
- Gloves and parkas worn by sentries only.
- One fried egg banjo per man per night, NO more.
- No structural alterations to your rooms.
- Don't wash puttees or pullovers in the washing machine, it gets clogged.
- Report damaged ammo.
- 15 gloves being issued per platoon.
- Don't mark flak jackets.
- Four syrettes of morphine per platoon.
- Keep the noise down in the accomm.

- Watch the chains on the gate, don't drive into them. If broken report. Watch your fingers.
- One external phone for general use is at the top of the emergency stairs. Don't break it if arguing with wife, girlfriend!
- If you want cheap cards see CQMS (33p for 12), not the wog man (15p each).
- Go Black if near 219 Springfield, they're getting jumpy and have a persecution complex.
- Check ammo dates, hand in any RG74 in for exchange. RG – Radway Green where it's made.
- Haircuts – Now!
- Cam cream to be worn at night now.
- Don't use glossy (porn?) mags as bog paper, they block the bogs. Ask for bog roll before!
- Dress in cookhouse is clean T-shirts and denims, no smelly singlets.
- Don't sit on the wog shop cooker to warm your arses.
- Vehicles must have their lights on at all times.
- Fill in VCP reports properly and legibly.
- Turn off hot taps.
- Volunteers wanted with full driving licence for driving in Berlin.
- Don't spray water around the showers, electrical point!
- Free cigarettes will be issued at Christmas.
- If your vehicle breaks down don't try to push it, call for a tow. Windscreens to remain up at all times.
- If you have a body on your hands don't give a statement to anyone until you have had legal advice from DALS (Director of army legal services).
- Use the complaints book sensibly.
- Exchange any stained mattresses.
- Don't bring stray dogs into the base.

- The door that was broken costs £41.50! Managed to get it down to £15, advance party to pay.
- Book early calls through the ops room.
- Don't belt kids for verbal abuse!
- Vehicle commanders get a grip of the RCT drivers, too many crashes. Don't speed.
- Only issue waterproofs to be worn.
- L/Cpl Gibbins… get your statement in tonight. Last warning.
- Drinking, don't exceed limits, no hoarding. Don't accept drinks from Prots.
- Don't jeer at funerals.
- The Adjutant (Capt. John Reith) having 'a number' of NDs at the unloading bay at TAC HQ.
- The CO (Lt. Col David Taylor) completely ignoring a cordon following an incendiary attack on Springfield Rd and walking through it.
- The CO insisting waterproofs were to be worn under smocks.
- I learnt how to break an egg with one hand to make banjos for the lads.
- I learnt how to beat the crap out of steak to tenderise it.
- Searches are never a waste of time.
- Room inspections.
- Do not remove your sling swivels.
- Don't ring RAF Aldergrove to change your flights, do it via CSM.
- Keep your feet off armchairs or you'll pay for cleaning.
- Stop taking fuses from the washing machine.
- Damaged door money to me by the 7th Jan!
- Do not visit pubs unless tasked to do so.
- Avoid drunks when on patrol.
- Don't use fire extinguishers to hold open doors.

- If the wog shop puts prices up tell the Colour Man. CQMS.
- Watch out for 'permanent send' on your radio.
- Cpl Emberson lost his ring in the washroom.
- Be nice to bus drivers.
- Don't crash stop vehicles.
- Don't reverse pigs without a guide. Someone go squashed in Flax St. Mill.
- Wear your ID discs.
- A milkman has complained that he had 60 bottle tops pushed in. Don't do it!
- RMP cannot order you to unload your weapon on the streets.
- New PARA smocks will be issued on return to UK!!
- Married and intend to marry blokes get your bids in for quarters in Berlin.
- Only piss in the bogs.
- Face veils must be worn.
- Kick Royal Anglian's arses if idle on patrol.
- Beer up by 1p per can.
- Watch kit security with Anglians around. 9 smocks already stolen in Echelon.
- Don't get caught painting slogans. It was L/Cpl Loxton from B Coy who was rather stupidly painting slogans: 'Pope is Airborne – Wears a Red Beret.'
- 0930 28 March leave ends, be back.
- Someone piss-stained Reid's mattress… he's in hospital!
- The covert OP that was compromised when one of the Toms fell through the floor of the loft into the room below.

PART 7

AFTER THE TOUR

2 PARA returned to Aldershot for post-tour leave and then moved to a two-year posting in Berlin.

I was posted from the Battalion to The Depot The Parachute Regiment and Airborne Forces to train recruits, a job I loved. Circumstances changed and I left the Regiment in 1979 to work with Halliburton in the offshore oil and gas industry but kept in touch by joining 15 (SV) Bn The Parachute Regiment. I was awarded the Territorial Decoration (TD) in 1996.

I finally gave up soldiering (as a Major in 1999) whilst working as a Watch Keeper/Liaison Officer in 5 Airborne Brigade.

My last military jump was into Arnhem in September 1999 for the 55th anniversary of the battle. A proud and moving event.

I travelled the world with the oil business and never looked back. My last job was as an Operations Superintendent working for BW Offshore on a Norwegian and Singapore based project to build the FPSO Catcher – Google it! She is now producing oil and gas in the UK sector. Retired in 2016. Had a new knee fitted in 2018. Happily married.

After Berlin 2 PARA was posted to Ballykinler in NI for a two-year accompanied tour during which they suffered the awful tragedy of the double explosion at Warrenpoint when 16 Paratroopers died alongside two Queens Own Highlanders.

In 1982 they went to the Falklands where sadly two of my soldiers from D Coy, Steve Prior and Paul Sullivan died at the Battle of Goose Green and Marty Madge was shot in the face and arm.

On the 10th April 1998 the Good Friday Agreement was signed which effectively put an end to "The Troubles". Operation Banner ended on 31st July 2007. Fingers crossed.

The Parachute Regiment received over 40 gallantry awards and 180 honours and commendations and 60 Mention in Despatches in this, the longest campaign in the history of Airborne Forces. 2 PARA was to spend 114 months in Northern Ireland across 16 tours conducted between 1970 to 2002, longer than any other Parachute Battalion.

763 members of the Armed Forces died as a result of terrorist activity during The Troubles and 6,116 known to have been wounded. 2 PARA lost 27 killed.

With thanks and respect and pride to all in The Parachute Regiment, in particular the men of 10 Platoon, D Company 2 PARA, who throughout our tours showed friendship, courage, restraint and professionalism. Without you I wouldn't be who I am today.

Utrinque Paratus.

TUESDAY JULY 25 1995

In Brief

Belfast army base goes

WORK began yesterday on demolishing the army's North Howard Street base in the Falls Road.

The run-down Victorian red-bricked former mill was the first army base established in the west Belfast area 25 years ago, and the first to be decommissioned following the IRA ceasefire 11 months ago.

The gap will be filled with several hundred yards of "peaceline" wall between the still divided Catholic and Protestant communities.

Where are we all today? April 2020.

David Ellis	Living in Aberdeenshire.
Don MacNaughton	Living in Aldershot. Seen on TV in 2019 having been 'milkshaked' whilst supporting the Brexit Party.
Don Elliott	Living in the Philippines.
Fred Squires	Living in Spain.
Gordon Fawcett	Living in Scotland.
Ian Taylor	Living in Germany.
John Bell	Living in Spain.
John Robinson	Demobbed in '83 after a 4-year tour in N Ireland then joined Derbyshire Police just in time for the miners' strike which was fun. Then went through CID, Regional/National Crime squads and retired fully in 2010 after two years in Afghanistan working with their drugs teams.
Keith Donkin	I completed a full career of 28 yrs in the Army. 1982 I transferred into the RAPTC Completed tours of RMAS, 1 PARA (first tour back after Bloody Sunday), Depot PARA. School of PT Sennelager, Glencorse, ATR Winchester, Bosnia. Commissioned – Captain. Living in Wiltshire.
Marty Magerison	After a posting to Berlin was promoted, demoted, sent to B Coy, Promoted and promoted to Cpl before leaving. Went to Ballykinler 20 months and involved with

the aftermath of Warrenpoint under
General Sir Mike Jackson, then Maj.
Was Cpl Sec Cmd B Coy 6 Pl under Lt
Chip Chapman (Now retired General). Maj
John Crossland was O.C. Was shot in the
face and arm at Goose Green.
Did BMATT posting Zimbabwe then did a
tour/posting to NITAT, and back to 2
PARA.
Served 2 tours of Depot, and 3 South
Armagh Tours and a 2-year residential in
Belfast Palace Barracks
Left as a WO2 in Dec 97, went into civvy
street, hated it, worked abroad on a variety
of contracts, Iraq 2003, Sudan, Bhutan,
Tanzania, divorced twice, been with
current 2 I/C 16 yrs, studied as a
counsellor in 2001-03. Now self-retired
and volunteer with veterans organisations
and do lots of golf and dog walking. Had 2
stents fitted in Jan 2019, continue to walk
and golf, babysit 3 grandchildren and enjoy
the planet whilst we can.

Michael Emberson — Continued to serve in 2 PARA until 1982
when he transferred to the Intelligence
Corps.
Leaving in 1990 he went on to a career in
the voluntary sector and is now retired and
living in Lincolnshire

Mick Gibbins — Living in Manchester and spotted in The
Brown Cow in Manchester.

Peter Akister — Semi-retired and living in Norwich.
I spent 1974-1977 in 2 PARA, left and

went to Depot PARA, followed by 1
PARA, IJLB, BMATT Zimbabwe, HQ
SEDIST. Left Army in 1986 and went to
Sri Lanka with KMS to run a Training
Team. In 1988 joined Norwich Union and
embarked on an HR career in Financial
Services and various Private/Public sector
organisations. Ran a TA Company 1988-
1992 in Norwich.

Rooster Barber	Living in Brecon.
Thomas Camp	Commissioned into the Royal Artillery in 1983. Retired as a colonel in 2005. Lives in France.
Warwick Stacey	Living in Sydney.
Nick O'Connor	Living in Australia.
Philip Russell	Retired and living in Beckenham.

In Valhalla.

Dave Smith 28	Rumoured to have died on Piper A platform but is not on the memorial roll.
Geoff Hough	Suicide. No more details.
Ian Bland	Died 2019.
Jimmy Kerr	Died 2015.
Paul Sullivan	Killed at Goose Green.
Steve Prior	Killed at Goose Green.

PART 8

HISTORY, TRAINING, KIT AND THE PEOPLE

Did we do a good job? Yes, I strongly believe that we did. I am sure that there are people alive today who would not be so were it not for the presence of the Regiment and the British Army in Ulster. Our job was to keep the peace, not solve the problem. We, the Army, were not perfect by any means; mistakes were made, crimes probably committed and of course the shadow of Bloody Sunday still hangs over the Regiment. I suspect that we, the PARAs, were both feared and respected by all sides. Sadly successful hits against us counted highly in kudos for the IRA, such is the price of fame. Warrenpoint being a terrible example.

Tours

In the 1970s Northern Ireland took up much of the Regiment's time. Tours were more or less four months long with a month or so of pre-tour training and at the end if you were lucky you got a few weeks end-of-tour leave. In addition there were the two-year accompanied tours based in such delightful places as Ballykinler or Palace Barracks. These were fully operational, however, families came to stay. I have heard mixed feelings about these. Moving your family into an alien and possibly hostile environment seems a bit strange to me, not something I have experienced though. Funnily enough it was never considered an option in Helmand!

Fitting in airborne exercises with NATO in Europe and the odd jolly to Malaysia, the USA and so on kept us all very busy, not to mention individual training courses in the UK and damp airborne exercises on Salisbury Plain, Otterburn and Sennybridge.

I imagine that nothing much changes even today. Nine-month tours in Afghanistan sounded pretty hellish. A shrinking Army does not help. At the height of the Troubles in 1972 there were about 27,000 soldiers in Ulster out of a total number of about 371,000. By 1977 the Army had shrunk to about 330,000. Today? About 81,500, not including reserves in all cases. We would struggle to cope if Ulster 'kicked off' again. I think Parachute battalions were on tour pretty much every year.

I thoroughly enjoyed my tours in Belfast. It was everything a young officer wanted – a buzz, an element of danger, command of the Toms; it was both boring (six hours on stag in the ops room) and exciting and you never knew what was round the corner. Was I ever scared? No, I don't recall ever being so. You're invincible in your 20s, especially when you're a Paratrooper! After the bomb attack we were a bit more twitchy perhaps, which I suppose is understandable. Do I get flashbacks etc? No. There are events that do stand out in my memory, particularly the explosion in North Howard Street, that is very vivid, but then we all have vivid memories of intense events. I'm glad I was there.

Other than a brief visit I did not serve on the border or in the country so I cannot comment on operations there nor make comparisons. I am sure there were different challenges in each area. In the city operational life was dominated by constant contact with the civilian population which meant that we acted as traffic wardens, police, counsellors, ambulance drivers, security guards, social workers and so on. Not stuff associated with being a Paratrooper. But the Army and the missions change.

Training

I believe that we were well enough trained for what we had to do. NITAT did a pretty decent job of training us in operations as well as explaining the history behind the whole miserable saga that was Northern Ireland in the 1970s. The Regiment had completed six tours by the time we went in '76 and as young men we all had to learn quickly and rely to an extent on the experiences of the Officers and NCOs, always to be taken with a pinch of salt! I was on the 1975 tour based at Flax St Mill so I wasn't totally green, also I had spent a while there in 1972 with the Royal Navy where I heard my first shot fired in anger, funnily enough by a Paratrooper in the Ballymurphy.

We carried out training locally in Aldershot, often using the Old Cavalry Barracks, for a few weeks, then deployed to the NITAT facilities at Hythe and Lydd in Kent. For those Battalions going into the country they went to SPTA (Stamford Practical Training Area) in Norfolk. NITAT trained us to cope with all situations:

- Routine urban patrolling techniques both on foot and in vehicles.
- Ops room routines.
- Vehicle Check Points.
- Personnel checks.
- Searching houses. We all received basic training in searching but selected bods went on more detailed Search Team courses and they became the Company Search Teams once deployed.
- Much time was spent on the ranges carrying out normal rifle shooting and the use of the Baton Round.
- The MUF range (Marksmanship Under Fire) was set up in an old Napoleonic fort and allowed soldiers to experience incoming fire from various types of ammunition whilst they were in a mock-up sangar. The idea being that they could identify HV and LV shots and even for the supermen to identify the type of round or weapon used against them.

- The other and most useful of ranges was a mock-up of a series of streets down which a patrol would proceed. The staff in a control tower could see the patrol and record their actions on CCTV for playback during the debrief. The control staff could activate pop up targets, both terrorist and civvy. Incoming fire and the strike of rounds was simulated by bangs and the patrol could return live fire at the targets. The SLRs were converted for this purpose to fire a .22 LR round to reduce noise and collateral damage. Similarly the staff could set off simulated IEDs. This range was not only a lot of fun but massively good training and such a change from the normal 'gravel belly' 300 meter ranges.

Riot control training at Hythe & Lydd.

Kit and Weapons

I hear of soldiers today complaining about the standard of their kit. All I would say is get dressed up in the stuff we had in the 1970s and go and mess about on the Sennybridge training area for three weeks in the winter. Enough said. Apart from the Dennison Smock obviously, which really was the dog's danglies. I still have mine and intend to be buried in it.

We were well enough equipped for the city. The Pye Pocketphone radios worked pretty well throughout the area and fitted neatly into the top pocket of our smocks.

We didn't carry much kit, usually a belt with an ammo pouch and maybe a water bottle was all we needed.

If stones got chucked steel PARA helmets, shields and the FRG (Federal Riot Gun – rubber bullets/baton rounds to you) were kept in the box in the back of the Rovers or Pigs. In the earlier tours the BR was the black 'rubber dick', by 1976 they were being replaced by the harder beige-coloured PVC number.

Berets were worn nearly always during my tours. I mentioned waterproofs, a good to have but rather silly I thought to wear them under smocks. Flak jackets were compulsory and we wore them over our smocks. I believe they were worn under smocks at one time to make the blokes look big and menacing.

The rifle we carried was the standard SLR (Self Loading Rifle) firing the 7.62mm NATO round. We carried a magazine of twenty rounds and were required to carry the weapon loaded but not 'made ready' i.e. one up the spout. Often the top round in the magazine was tracer, a useful item for target indication. We were not allowed bayonets though they were issued right at the beginning of the Troubles. Some officers, the CO and Adjutant among others, carried the standard Browning 9mm pistol, everyone else carried the SLR. It packed a good punch, was easily capable of penetrating the walls of the Victorian houses predominant in Belfast and it made a fine noise. It was longer than the current SA80 version and we found this to be useful when using the butt to show people the error of their ways. A sling was attached to the rear sling swivel and a loop was passed around the wrist in order to reduce the likelihood of someone grabbing the rifle.

GPMGs (machine guns) were deployed at the beginning of the Troubles and were used in the country, however, we were not allowed to use them on the streets and quite rightly so.

In addition, held at base, was the trusty 84mm Carl Gustav Anti-Tank Gun, known as the Charlie G. This was to be used on a remote fire contraption and would fire a TPTP (target practice tracer projectile, i.e. it didn't go bang when it hit the target). This was to be used in extremis against suspected car bombs if ATO couldn't make it. I don't recall ever hearing of one being used in anger though there was an ND (negligent discharge) with one by HM Royal Marines whilst carrying out drills at Girdwood Park base. They used a TPTP instead of an inert drill round. I'm told it went through several walls and disturbed a number of Marines trying to sleep. The noise and back blast from these weapons was pretty impressive. The Army Book of Excuses doesn't have a paragraph to explain this cock-up. Perhaps the Royal Marines do.

The NCOs & Toms

It was brilliant working with the Platoon; all ranks were, and still are, a never ending source of support, amusement and wicked humour mixed with the ability to take the piss – especially from young officers. They were loyal, friendly, intelligent (mostly!) and imbued with what we were taught as recruits… ABI – Airborne Initiative. To this day I have kept in touch with soldiers and officers whose friendship I first made and valued in the 1970s. I doubt that there are many walks of civilian life where this would be the case. Good on you, Facebook!

We should never forget the really important role played by the Junior

NCOs. This campaign was theirs. They were in command on the ground most of the time. Life and death situations were theirs to control. As junior officers we had to place our trust in them and hardly ever did they fail. I had enormous support and friendship with my NCOs and it is something that I shall never forget.

The senior NCOs, in particular the Platoon Sergeants, were for the junior officers the font of all knowledge. They advised, bollocked, helped and took the piss out of young officers and thank goodness for them.

The standard of NCOs of all ranks in the Regiment was and remains high. They excelled themselves in Northern Ireland, the Falklands, Iraq and Afghanistan.

The Senior Officers

The commanders at Company and Battalion level, despite my criticisms, were with one or two exceptions pretty good. They were under a different sort of pressure than us lower forms of life. In general we were given tasks, guided, and then left to get on with it as we saw fit. Interference from above was, by and large, minimal and thanks for that. We knew what to do and were trusted and we were damned good at our job. I think most junior officers adopted the same process for their blokes: brief them for the mission, ensure they know what they have to do, give them the tools and support that they need and then let them get on with it.

Of course from time to time things did not always go as planned but on this particular tour we carried out the mission with efficiency, humanity and humour.

I did not find the CO an easy man to deal with and we had several frank discussions. I believe that he disliked me, maybe as a result of my continual misdemeanours (with Simon Barry) whilst at Sandhurst in 73/74 where he was the Chief Instructor as a Major. Such is life. I hope that, should we ever meet again he would buy me a pint. His edict on waterproofs was ridiculous, he wore cam cream despite it being forbidden by Bn HQ. I don't think he was well respected in the Battalion.

Maj. Ben Hodgson, my Company Commander, who I really liked, wrote my annual confidential report in 1977 which was pretty damn good. Taylor overrode it and gave me a poor one. I refused to sign it. The Adjutant (John Reith) sent the whole thing to Regimental HQ in Aldershot who made Taylor re write it pretty much as Ben had.

The Locals & PIRA

As with most societies it only takes a few to ruin the lives of the rest. I do not intend to attempt to go into the history and the reasons behind the Troubles other than to say that the British Government were pretty remiss in dealing with what were in many cases reasonable gripes by the Catholic community. Such mistakes as Internment without trial and of course Bloody Sunday really played into the hands of PIRA and thereafter their numbers increased dramatically. Once PIRA emerged there was to be no going back for many years to come.

I spoke to many locals during personnel checks on the streets, during house searches or in pubs and shops. I found most of the older people delightful as the Irish are. None wanted the fear, destruction, corruption and uncertainty that was life then. Many people said thank you for being here and I know that they meant it. There were acts of kindness but care had to be taken when doing so. There were informers and very bad people who regarded such behaviour as treachery. I felt so sad for the normal people of Belfast, especially the children who knew no other life.

Our area was almost 100% Catholic/Republican, though whilst by no means all of them supported PIRA they certainly did have some sympathy for their cause which was a United Ireland. PIRA's methods of intimidation and criminality were not universally supported but there was little that the average citizen could do about it. There were a few brave souls who informed against PIRA and God help them if they were caught. PIRA (and indeed the Prot organisations) showed no mercy to 'touts'. Think yourself lucky if you got away with a beating or kneecapping. Kneecapping with a Black & Decker drill bought a whole new meaning to the word terror! They held age and sex as no barrier to torture and murder; there are still a number of 'The Disappeared' yet to be found.

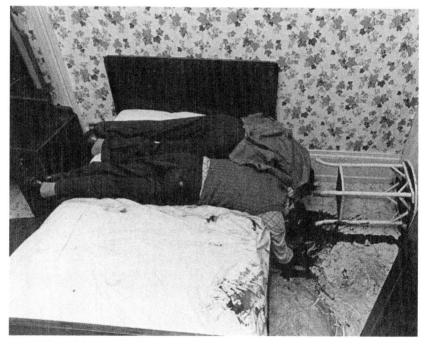

"Nutted". Two head jobs. Why? Wrong religion, wrong place at the wrong time, said the wrong thing, who knows?

I had no respect for PIRA, or the Loyalist gangs either. They were brutal, cowardly thugs. They killed men, women and children many were random killings involving bombs and booby traps. They ruined tens of thousands if not hundreds of thousands of lives and gained nothing. I cannot find any official record of those wounded or mutilated. For the British Labour Government to have given an amnesty to murderers whilst pursuing old soldiers is disgraceful.

According to Malcolm Sutton's Index of Deaths from the Conflict in Ireland, of those killed by Republican paramilitaries:

1080 (52.5%) were members or former members of the British Security Forces.

721 (35.1%) were civilians.

188 (9.2%) were members of republican paramilitaries.

57 (2.8%) were members of loyalist paramilitaries.

11 (0.5%) were members of the Irish Security Forces.

In general I suppose that Belfast was a mirror image of many of the run-down British cities on the mainland in the 60s and 70s. Crap housing, unemployment, petty crime (PIRA would punish unauthorised crime! Pot – kettle – black!) and social inequality all played their part in fermenting unrest.

In my time there the drug trade had not really kicked off; though there were users the problem was not considered to be a big issue. If it had been, PIRA et al would have got stuck in to make money as I presume they did later on in the conflict.

The standard of housing varied from brand new to Victorian back-to-back terraces with a shitty alley between. The Divis Flats, just outside our TAOR, was a large block which was built in 1966 and named after Belfast's Divis Mountain. During the Troubles, the British Army built an observation post on top of the tower.

The flats were the centre of much IRA activity throughout the Troubles. Rioters would entice soldiers to give chase into an arena from which their fighting could be viewed by hundreds of people on the balconies. Joyriders used the space in the same way, to perform before an audience.

The bin men weren't keen on certain areas for fear of hijacking. As mentioned earlier outside privies were not uncommon. Searching these houses was to me, a middle-class bloke from a good family, and many of the lads a bit of an eye-opener. Some houses were immaculate, others less so. Bottles of piss, soiled underwear, used Tampax lying around and even the odd jobby were not uncommon. We were probably fortunate in only being infested with fleas on one occasion.

The one thing that will forever remind me of those days in Belfast is the smell of coal fires. Especially on a damp winter's eve.

One day I may go back and see if much has changed. I hope it has, then our time there would not have been wasted.

We were a force for good.

The Parachute Regiment & Airborne Forces Memorial.

From 'Visor' Service News for Northern Ireland. 11ᵗʰ March 1977.
2 PARA Unit Feature.

Dedicated to the memory of two brave men.
Paul Sullivan & Stephen Prior.

ABOUT THE AUTHOR

David Ellis joined the Royal Navy as an Officer Cadet in 1970 and first went to Belfast whilst a Midshipman serving in HMS *Kellington,* patrolling off the coast of the Province on anti-gun-running duties.

He joined The Parachute Regiment in 1973, and served with D Company 2 PARA as a rifle platoon commander and later as an instructor at The Depot The Parachute Regiment & Airborne Forces. He left the Regular Army in 1979 and joined the Territorial Army in 1983 serving with The Parachute Regiment until retiring as a Major in 1999. He was awarded the Territorial Decoration in 1996.

After leaving the Regular Army he worked in the oil and gas industry on and offshore worldwide until retiring in 2016.

He is married and lives in Aberdeenshire.